Old Testament Theology and the Rest of God

Old Testament Theology and the Rest of God

Nicholas Haydock

WIPF & STOCK · Eugene, Oregon

Wipf & Stock
An Imprint of Wipf and Stock Publishers
199 W. 8th Ave., Suite 3
Eugene, OR 97401

www.wipfandstock.com

PAPERBACK ISBN: 978-1-4982-2996-8
HARDCOVER ISBN: 978-1-4982-2998-2

Manufactured in the U.S.A.

Scripture taken from the NEW AMERICAN STANDARD BIBLE®, © Copyright 1960, 1962, 1963, 1968, 1971, 1972, 1973, 1975, 1977, 1995 by The Lockman Foundation. Used by permission.

Contents

Acknowledgments

This book was written during a time of waiting and trusting in God. Its completion would not be possible without the encouragement and support I received from many, most notably that given to me by my parents and church family. I also gratefully give thanks for the kindness, generosity and fellowship shown to me by my good friend Wendy Barber, throughout my time of researching the topic.

Like the longing and waiting of the Church, mine own ability to wait is merely a testimony to God's grace and goodness. To him be praise and thanks.

Introduction

The concept of God's rest lies at the heart of the Old Testament's message. It is the hope of God's word being fulfilled and it is the outcome of putting hope in the word of God. It provides a story into which a faithful Israelite must imagine himself and it provides a message of good news for all peoples.

For many the claim that "rest lies at the heart of the Old Testament's message" will cause a sense of bewilderment as they struggle to recollect texts where the subject of rest even comes up. Yet even a brief survey highlights the fact that the theme of "rest" repeatedly occurs at key moments in the text; from creation through to God's covenant with David, from great messianic prophecies through to the construction of Solomon's temple, from Noah through to the conquest of the land; rest is seen to be a prominent theme.

In addition to this, it should be recognized that the nations which surrounded Israel held to worldviews which were prominently marked by a supposed ongoing struggle between "rest" and "chaos." One would expect to find evidence in the Old Testament either of Israel sharing this worldview, of Israel fighting against these opposing worldviews, or a mixture of both, signaling a struggle within the community.

This study attempts to show firstly that Israel held one coherent theology of rest, which was distinct from that held by the surrounding nations. Secondly the study hopes to convince the reader that "rest" comprised a significant part of Israel's message for the nations.

It will become immediately clear to the reader that the biblical concept of rest goes beyond merely the cessation of work, of being refreshed or of having peace and quiet. A working definition for the Old Testament notion of rest, though certainly including these things also goes beyond them. It is here defined as "having a holistic state of being, freely given by God in accordance to his word."

Rest is "a holistic state of being;" this alludes to the fact that rest is the experience of God's creation prior to the fall. For the Israelite, the opportunities for rest offered in this life point primarily to the eternal rest when creation is restored to its Edenic state.

Rest is "freely given by God;" it is God who gives rest and it is given because God chooses to give it. Within the worldviews of the surrounding nations, rest was understood to be something attained through earning the favor of the gods. In the Old Testament though, God is consistently seen to offer his rest freely to all who will turn to him.

Rest is given "according to God's word;" it is impossible in defining "rest" to divorce it from God's own word, because the two are so intimately connected. Rest is both the fruit of obedience to God's word, and it is the subject of hope, being assured by the fact that God promised it.

Rest in the World of Old Testament Theology

Old Testament theology has typically paid little attention to the concept of rest and it is not uncommon for a huge volume on the subject to make no or scant reference to the topic. The reason for this absence is not altogether clear; perhaps it is only that interest has been focused elsewhere, but it is also possible that this neglect is aided by the fact that the prominence of "rest" in the ancient Near Eastern mindset is not shared by the modern western world.

There are two noteworthy exceptions to this dearth of analysis. First of all, an essay written on the subject by von Rad,[1] who supposed there to be competing understandings and applications concerning this rest throughout the Old Testament corpus.

Second is an article written by Water Kaiser;[2] Kaiser sees the concept of rest as a point of continuity between the Old and New Testaments and in contrast to von Rad supposes that there is a unified witness to the theme of rest in the Bible. Kaiser of course understands the theme of "promise" as central to the Old Testament message and his interest in rest stems from this; he sees the promise of rest as one strand of the Old Testament message as he traces the theme through Joshua and Psalm 95 to the book of Hebrews.

These two articles represent two very different approaches to the subject; either rest carries a variety of different meanings or it conveys one essential idea consistently throughout the canon.[3] Given the fact that the Old Testament was written and compiled over the course of many centuries, in different contexts and by numerous generations living under varying socio-political environments, the onus might seem to be on those who wish to show that there is a theology of rest which transcends the Old Testament. In response, this study will firstly try to trace how the theology of rest developed and progressed through the different stages in Israel's history. Secondly the study will argue that the essence of this theology remained the same throughout as evidenced by the consistent way God's rest relates to his word. On each of these two points a few things need to be said.

This study attempts to trace the understanding and development of "rest" through the various stages of Israel's history. This in itself is not controversial; there are aspects of a worldview which

1. Gerhard von Rad, *The Problem of the Hexateuch and Other Essays.*

2. Kaiser Jr., "The Promise Theme and the Theology of Rest."

3. Note that this issue is not being set up as a liberal versus evangelical debate. It is of course entirely possible for an evangelical Christian to hold that the word "rest" is used and understood differently in different contexts and vice versa.

transcend time and the changes of culture. Indeed it is widely considered that the struggle between rest and chaos remained prominent in the ancient Mesopotamian worldview throughout various stages of history. So if it can be shown that rest plays a significant role in the Yahwistic worldview then the hypothesis is entirely plausible.

The controversy comes however in the dating of texts. Indeed many treat such an exercise as either futile or a distraction from the important task of studying the texts in the canonical form in which they have been passed down. In response, it is good firstly to affirm the place and importance of the canonical interpretation of scripture, yet this does not make a diachronical approach to scripture inappropriate. In fact it makes the task of diachronical study imperative, for the canon itself repeatedly emphasizes that Israel's faith is markedly historical; pointing to God's past deeds and revelation as the source for current and future hope.[4]

This study builds upon a wealth of literature which affirms the historical reliability underpinning the Old Testament texts. Throughout the course of study and where appropriate arguments will be cited regarding the dating of texts, in order to demonstrate the essential continuity of the Old Testament's theology of rest, and respond to certain presuppositions held by those supposing there to be multiple theologies of rest.

The cornerstone of the argument is that the Israel's single coherent theology of rest is attested to by its consistent relationship with "God's word."

The question of whether or not there is indeed also only one theology of God's word is too large to be attended to here and is deserving of its own space. Yet by way of a brief comment; the existence of the canon itself would indicate a shared view on the importance of God's word and as a collected body it supposedly has a singular vision and purpose.

4. Historically, commendable attempts at doing Old Testament theology which are both canonical and diachronical, while holding to conservative convictions have been offered by the likes of Gerhard Vos, Chester Lehman, Walter Kaiser, Elmer Martens, Barton Payne and Eugene Merrill, and provide good precedent for this comparatively meagre study.

The Language of Rest

Ideas do not always crystallize into words and it is well to remember this here. The concept of "rest" in Israel's worldview cannot be tied to any one word. More than this, the goal here is not to ascribe meanings to particular words, but rather to explore the meanings of these words in the context of Scripture, in as much as they relate to the broader theological concept of "rest."

Having said this, there are a number of Hebrew words can be translated into English as "rest" and central among them is the verb *nuah*. Linked here linguistically to the verbal root of *nuah* are the words *menoah* "resting place" and *nahalah* meaning "inheritance." The conceptual link between these words is most clearly evidenced in Deuteronomy:

> You shall not do at all what we are doing here today, every man doing whatever is right in his own eyes; for you have not as yet come to the resting place and the inheritance which the Lord your God is giving you. When you cross the Jordan and live in the land which the Lord your God is giving you to inherit, and He gives you rest from all your enemies around you so that you live in security.
>
> Deuteronomy 12:8–10

The analysis of this passage and others cited here in the introduction will be explored more fully in the course of the study. Here though it is important to notice that this passage clearly shows that the semantic range of *nuah* rightfully extends so far as to include the notion of possessing an inheritance.

Also closely associated with *nuah* are the verbs *shabat* "to cease" or "to rest" and *shaqat* normally translated "rest" with the sense of not having war. These two verbs do not overlap with each other in terms of meaning, yet both seem to hold some exchange with the word *nuah*.

To begin with *shabat*, the main reason for taking this together with *nuah* is the fourth commandment:

> Remember the sabbath day, to keep it holy. Six days you
> shall labor and do all your work, but the seventh day is
> a sabbath of the Lord your God; in it you shall not do
> any work, you or your son or your daughter, your male
> or your female servant or your cattle or your sojourner
> who stays with you. For in six days the Lord made the
> heavens and the earth, the sea and all that is in them, and
> rested on the seventh day; therefore the Lord blessed the
> sabbath day and made it holy.

Exodus 20:8–11

In the Genesis account God rests (*shabat*) yet in this text the people of God are told to cease from their work because God rested (*nuah*) on the seventh day.

Similarly there is also good reason to associate *shaqat* with the concept of rest. The most explicit reference in favor of this is 2 Chronicles 20:30, "and the kingdom of Jehoshaphat was at peace (*shaqat*), for his God had given him rest (*nuah*) on every side". Here the rest from war is indicative of God's rest *nuah*.

The point to take from this brief survey is that there is a conceptual link between *nuah* and these other words, at least in certain contexts. Of course these words can and do have a semantic range beyond the interests of this study and so attention must carefully be given to the context in which they are found.

With these introductory remarks being made, attention now turns to the study itself, beginning with the creation account and story of Noah which are amongst the earliest writings in the Old Testament.

Chapter 1

Creation and God's Rest

This chapter will explore the concept of rest in the creation narrative. It is not exhaustive because the proceeding chapters will often take up observations made in this chapter, exploring creation's relationship with for example the tabernacle or the land. Yet it is necessary to consider Gen. 1–3 on its own merit, namely because it is reasonable to think that the source of the creation narrative has an early date preceding other texts which draw upon it.

God's Eternal Rest

When considering Gen. 1 it is important to appreciate that "rest" is not just something God does, or the absence of him doing anything on the seventh day. Rest is the culmination and purpose of his creative activity.

Gen. 1—2:3 is a structured account of how God created the world, which displays a significant amount of repetition in language. The first six days in particular fit a common pattern: God speaks, it happens, God sees that it is good and there is evening and morning. This pattern though is broken with the account of the seventh day.

> Thus the heavens and the earth were completed, and all their hosts. By the seventh day God completed His work which He had done, and He rested on the seventh day from all His work which He had done. Then God blessed

the seventh day and sanctified it, because in it He rested
from all His work which God had created and made.

Genesis 2:1–3

Whereas the first six days always end with the formula "and there
was evening and there was night," this formula is notably absent
from the seventh day. There is no creative activity on the seventh
day, but rather God ceases from it because it was finished and he saw
that it was very good. Note also that in the account itself, God marks
the seventh day out because he blesses it and makes it holy. For this
reason it is possible to talk of the seven days being, six plus one.

The six plus one literary- structure, observable in Gen. 1—2:3
has also been observed elsewhere in the ancient world. Notably in
the Gilgamesh epic with the flood which lasts for six days, in the
Enuma Elish epic where for six days the horns are shining before
the seventh and also within some of the Ugaritic epics such as the
Aqhat epic where Daniel offers sacrifices for seven days and on the
seventh he brings his prayer before the god El. In all of these cases
the six plus one literary structure served to emphasize the seventh.
It was an ancient Semitic device extending far back into the cultural
memory of the region and would have been readily recognisable[1].
Even still, the employment of it in Genesis is unique, as no other
ancient Near Eastern account develops a narrative for each day.[2]

In looking specifically at the Genesis account, the narrative
seems to anticipate the seventh day which is depicted as being the
culmination of God's creative work. For example it has been often
noted that the opening, "in the beginning God created the heavens
and the earth," is composed of seven Hebrew words. The number
seven features prominently throughout the passage in that a number of phrases such as "let there be," "and it was so" and "and God
made" occur seven times. This all culminates in Gen. 2:2–3 where
the fact that it is the seventh day is repeated; unlike the other days
and that the Hebrew nicely fits four lines of seven words.[3]

1. Young, *Studies in Genesis One*, 79.
2. Loewenstamm, "The Seven Day-Unit in Ugaritic Epic Literature," 132.
3. Matthews, *Genesis 1–11:26*, 176.

As already noted, the seventh day lacks the familiar ending "and there was evening and there was night." It has been widely recognized, that in a sense then the seventh day is perpetual, at least until being interrupted by sin.[4] This is more than just an argument from silence, the other six days end with this formula and it would provide an obvious conclusion to this part of the creation account, so its absence is justifiably notable. On this matter, there is a natural overlap between the seventh day and the hoped for eschatological rest to come after a recreation, whereby the seventh day in Gen. 2 also serves to prefigure the eternal rest to come. In truth the association of Sabbath with eternity is an ancient one.[5] For instance the apocryphal *Life of Adam and Eve* states that "the seventh day is the sign of the resurrection and the world to come."[6] More importantly though, the Old Testament writings justify such a reading, as shall be noted in the course of the study.

Perhaps for some, an eschatological reading of the seventh day might appear to be speculative, but when consideration is given to the way in which the creation narrative is used elsewhere in the Pentateuch, keeping the eschatological hope on the interpretive horizon becomes not only defendable but necessary for understanding the theology of the Pentateuch as a coherent whole. The land which the Israelites were entering in to possess is painted using Edenic imagery and language and for generations after the conquest is remembered as an event still to come (e.g. Ps. 95:11). The tabernacle and the temple are framed by the story of Eden and point forward to a time when the Lord will come again and bring judgment and restoration. The story of Noah also points forward to a re-creation to come, as shall be seen in the next chapter. These are ideas which must be explored in more detail, yet the cumulative weight of evidence linking rest and the seventh day with re-creation after the *eschaton*, is substantial.

4. Ibid.

5. Heschel, *The Sabbath*, 73.

6. Charles, *The Apocrypha and Pseudopigrapha of the Old Testament: Volume 2*, 2:151.

Purpose and Provenance

Gen. 1–11 is not the only primeval proto-history from the ancient world which has been preserved to this day. In addition to Gen. 1–11 there is also the Sumerian king list, the Atrahasis epic and Eridu genesis. These all follow the basic pattern of creation, flood and a new start. The fact is that these kinds of narratives were not constructed after about 1600 BC, so it is reasonable to conclude that Gen. 1–11 at the very least goes back to the patriarchal period.[7]

The commonly held view that Gen. 1–11 is a redaction combining two sources, "J" which possibly held this triadic pattern of creation, flood and new start, with "P" written significantly later in the time of the exile, is unlikely simply because there is no reason why an exilic redactor should restrict himself to so faithfully adhering to the triadic pattern of "J."[8]

Linked to the above discussion is the idea that Genesis actually preserves two creation accounts: Gen. 1—2:4a composed in the exile and Gen. 2:4b—3:24 coming from "J." The primary reason given for distinguishing between the two is the use of the Hebrew word *toledot* in Gen. 2:4.[9] The word *toledot*, meaning these are "the generations of" appears eleven times altogether in the book of Genesis; introducing various sections and giving the book its overall structure. It is a mistake though to think that a *toledot* only introduces a new section. As can be seen by its use in Num. 3 and in the last chapter of Ruth, it is better described as acting like a hinge which connects what went before with what follows.[10] As a result, the book of Genesis can be seen to be made up of twelve sections joined together by these eleven *toledot* references. This understanding also best makes sense of the text of Gen. 1–3, as both sides of the *toledot* seem to a certain extent to parallel each other, indicating their essential unity.[11]

---

7. Kitchen, *On the Reliability of the Old Testament*, 426.

8. Garrett, *Rethinking Genesis*, 187.

9. Fretheim, *Creation, Fall and Flood*, 45.

10. Garrett, *Rethinking Genesis*, 33.

11. See Doukhan, *Genesis Creation Story*. Doukhan argues for a sevenfold

The creation narrative as a unified account dates back at least to the patriarchs and then it was worked in to the wider work of Genesis and the Pentateuch by Moses. So how then does the creation account in Genesis function within the wider context of the Pentateuch? A number of observations can be made: firstly it reveals God's character to the reader and outlines his intention for creation. Secondly, it provides a basis for observing the Sabbath day and lastly it sets the scene for the story which follows. The following paragraphs explore these three points respectively.

What does this text reveal about God? God is a God of love yet he judges sin, he creates but not for any selfish motive, he provides Adam with a helper because he cares for him and gives Adam and Eve commands for their own benefit. God carefully orders his creation, he is emotionally involved with it and is pained by humanity's rebellion. He is the all powerful creator who alone created the cosmos out of nothing, yet walks in the garden. The creation narrative reveals much of God's character, and these observations are only heightened when Genesis is contrasted with the creation myths of the surrounding nations. Notably in the literature of the surrounding nations, the gods' purpose in creating humanity is to carry the burden of the gods' workload, which contrasts sharply with the function given to Adam and Eve, that of ruling over and being stewards of God's creation. Further comparison will be considered in the chapter "Rest for the Nations," where the myths of the nations are considered in more detail.

The relationship between creation and Sabbath requires extensive analysis, which will be explored later. At this point though, it should be noted that although Gen. 1—2:3 doesn't actually use the noun Sabbath, it is implied. In Gen 2:3 the reader is told that God rested (*shabat*) or ceased on the seventh day and significantly, that God sanctified it and made that day holy. For this reason it is right to view Gen. 1—2:3 as providing an ordinance for Sabbath observance.[12] However it would not be right to limit the scope of

---

structure of Gen. 2:4–24 which parallels Gen. 1–2:4.

12. Cole, "The Sabbath and Genesis 2:1–3," 7.

the text to that function because the concept of God's rest extends beyond the Sabbath.

Gen. 1—2:3 sets the scene for the story which follows. This story is rooted in this theme of rest and never strays too far away from it. The Pentateuch may well be described as providing the historical basis for the Israelites' faith but it also provides the beginning of their story and gives a projected outline of the course it will take. Just as every story has a beginning it also has an end, so it would be foolish to think that the beginning of this story was written without paying attention to the final destination of the narrative.

Of course for the early Israelites in the desert, a prominent ending is imagined as entering into the land of rest. Yet there is another sense in which this does not complete the story, there are too many strands which are not tied up in such an ending, such as the prophet who is to come, the seed of the woman who will reverse the fall or the choosing of the mountain of God's inheritance before which the nations will tremble. It is necessary therefore to speak of projected "endings" which all point to the one ending. As shall be observed though, all these imagined endings refer back to the beginning of the story and the rest still to come which brings God's creation and his recreation together.

God's Word and God's Rest

It is frequently pointed out that God spoke creation into being, but considering the emphasis of the seventh day in Gen. 1–2:3, what is the relationship between God's rest and his word?

Rest is the fruit of God's word, existing when God's word has achieved what it was meant to achieve. Contrary to any person's sinful intentions and contrary to the worldview of the nations that surrounded Israel, rest is not the achievement of human activity but the fruit solely of God's word. What then does God say in the creation narrative? He *commands*, he *provides* and he *reveals*:

God both *commands* the world into being and he commands humanity to be fruitful, to fill the earth and subdue it, and to rule over his creation. Crucially, he also commands them not to eat of the tree of the knowledge of good and evil. Adam and Eve continue to enjoy God's rest so long as they obey God's word. When they disobey they are removed from the garden and implicit within this is the notion that they no longer enjoy God's rest but must toil. This contrast, between the toil and God's rest is made explicit in the naming of Noah, as shall be seen in the next chapter.

God *provides*; he gives to Adam and Eve sustenance both before and after the fall. Just as the world came to be through his word so also the assurance of God's provision is based on the fact that he speaks to promise it.

Lastly God *reveals* himself through his word. It is a literary characteristic of Semitic literature that a person's character is revealed by what they say. As opposed to contemporary western literature for example where the narrator informs the reader by describing the details of how something is said or the body language and dress of the speaker, in Old Testament narrative it is the spoken word which achieves this.[13] In Gen. 2:18 God says "it is not good for the man to be alone, I will make a helper suitable for him." It is not so much that God is an external processor but rather that in speaking, God's character, emotions, and motivations are revealed. Obviously, this aspect of God's speech is not distinct from his commands or his words of provision, but it is a point that deserves its own attention.

What was the significance of God's word for the ancient Hebrews? They believed also that they would enter into God's rest through obeying God's word, that they would be sustained by the promise of God's word and that through meditating on God's word, God would continue to reveal himself to them despite their being fallen human beings.

13. Alter, *The Art of Biblical Narrative.*

Chapter 2

Noah

The story of Noah contains many points of contact, connecting it with the creation narrative. One of its key functions for this study is that it demonstrates that the fall entailed the interruption of God's rest, something posited in the previous chapter when commenting on the absence of the "and there was evening and there was morning" formula, an interruption which can only be reinstated through an act of re-creation. This idea was also alluded to in the previous chapter, where it was suggested that the Old Testament holds to an eschatology rooted in the notion of a re-creation restoring God's rest. The story of Noah is just one piece of evidence for this.

The Naming of Noah

> Lamech lived one hundred and eighty-two years, and became the father of a son. Now he called his name Noah, saying, "This one will give us rest from our work and from the toil of our hands arising from the ground which the Lord has cursed." Then Lamech lived five hundred and ninety-five years after he became the father of Noah, and he had other sons and daughters. So all the days of Lamech were seven hundred and seventy-seven years, and he died.
>
> Genesis 5:28–31

The name of Noah is affiliated most clearly to the Hebrew word for "rest" *nuah*. Yet this passage does something quite surprising; when Lamech explains the reason for Noah's name he exclaims he will give us relief or comfort *yenahamenu* rather than he will give us rest *yenihenu*.[1] This leads to the question, how does the story of Noah leave the reader with a presentation of a comforted humanity?

A number of commentators such as Speiser,[2] von Rad,[3] and Westermann,[4] argue that the comfort came through the vineyard in Gen. 9:20 and the production of wine. One of the reasons behind this supposition is the sentiment that the flood which brought so much death could not be the focus of this comfort. Yet it should be recognized that on numerous occasions in the Old Testament, God's judgment of evil is seen as a source of comfort for Israel.

The text itself suggests that the comfort relates in some way to relief from the Adamic curse. Both Adam (Gen. 2:5) and Noah (Gen. 9:20) are described as workers of the ground, and in both stories the land is cursed because of man; in Gen. 3:17 because of Adam's sin and in Gen. 8.21 God promises not to curse the ground again "because of man."[5] This view is supported further by recognizing the play on words between "comfort" and the Lord "grieving" humanity's sin (Gen. 6:6) which are from the same verb root, *naham*. The note on the *nephilim* and humanity's sin which introduces the flood narrative, also echoes the account of the fall by using the words "beautiful," "saw," and "took," thereby making a direct link between the fall and the sinful state of humanity at the

1. Some have taken this to be a scribal mistake, as for example the translators of the Septuagint did, who amended it to read "he will give us rest." Given the play on the word *nuah* throughout the narrative, this conclusion might be tempting. Nevertheless, aside from the Septuagint there are no textual variants in favor of this reading and arguably there is also a play on words between "comfort" and the Lord being "grieved" in Gen. 6:6 where the same verb *naham* in the niphil conveys the means to be grieved.

2. Speiser, *Genesis*, 61.

3. von Rad, *Genesis*, 136.

4. Westermann, *Genesis 1–11*, 360.

5. Davies, "Sons of Cain," 36.

time of the flood.[6] The flood therefore brings comfort by bringing so much of humanity's sinfulness to an end.

For what reason though does Lamech say that Noah will "comfort us" as opposed to saying he will bring God's rest? Comfort occurs elsewhere in Genesis (Gen. 24:67, 27:42, 37:35, 38:12 and 50:21); in most of these references comfort relates to mourning, except for the last where Joseph "reassures" his brothers of his ongoing kindness to them, despite their father Jacob's death.[7] Perhaps reassurance is the best way to understand this comfort; Noah is a reassurance and comfort because he points to God's judgment on sin, God's continued involvement in his creation and that God's eternal rest will be restored through an act of re-creation following God's judgment on sin. This becomes evident upon close examination of the narrative.

Rest in the Story of Noah

The story of Noah under the scrutiny of source criticism was consistently viewed as the amalgamation of two sources; an early source named "J" and a source dating to the time of the exile "P." Yet this was partly a result of overlooking and misunderstanding the artistry behind Old Testament narrative and the function of repetition within it. The unity of the narrative is clearly evidenced by its chiastic literary structure.[8]

A^1 7 days waiting for the flood (Gen. 7:4)

A^2 7 days waiting for the flood (Gen. 7:10)

B 40 days of flood (Gen. 7:17)

C 150 days the waters prevail (Gen. 7:24)

C' 150 days the waters abate (Gen. 8:3)

B' 40 days the waters recede (Gen. 8:6)

6. Matthews, *Genesis 1–11:26*, 321.

7. Brueggemann, *Genesis*, 70.

8. Wenham, "The Coherence of the Flood Narrative," 437.

$A^{1'}$ 7 days of waiting (Gen. 8:10)

$A^{2'}$ 7 days of waiting (Gen. 8:12)

Further evidence for the narrative's unity can be observed in its interest in the theme of "rest" and the play on the word *nuah* throughout the passage, spanning both of the sections traditionally ascribed to the two sources "J" and "P."

The story of the flood is placed within the context both of humanity's sin and God's pain. Whereas man plots evil in his heart (Gen. 6:5), God is grieved and his heart is pained (Gen. 6:6). God's pain is similarly felt by Lamech who longs for an end to the painful toil resulting from the fall, an indication that Lamech's hopes are in line with the creator's disappointment.[9] In the midst of this setting, Noah finds favor in the Lord's eyes. The word for favor, *hen*, is an inversion of the consonants which make up Noah's name and constitute the first of many plays on Noah's name.[10]

Noah is commissioned to build the ark which of course he does just as the Lord commands him to. Then Noah and his family wait for God's word to be fulfilled, for which they must wait for a period of seven days (Gen. 7:4). The floods rise and then when they begin to recede, the ark comes to "rest" on the top of Mount Ararat (Gen. 8:4), another widely recognized play on Noah's name. Noah sends out a dove, but it finds no "resting place" (Gen. 8:9) so it returns and Noah waits a further seven days.

After the flood waters eventually recede, they exit the ark and Noah builds an altar on which he offers burnt offerings which come to God as a "pleasing aroma," *reah hannihoah*, another allusion to the name of Noah where God's wrath is appeased upon smelling the "pleasing aroma;" which might as Hamilton chooses to do, be translated, "rest inducing."[11] The question as to the most appropriate translation need not be of concern here, but this idea linking God's rest with his wrath is very important. God's rest can only be enjoyed once his wrath towards sin is appeased.

9. Cassuto, *From Adam to Noah*, 303.

10. Sasson, "Word-Play in Genesis 6:8–9," 165.

11. Hamilton, *Book of Genesis: Chapters 1–17*, 308.

Noah and the Re-creation

The story of Noah is told in such a way that it echoes and interacts with the story of creation. Indeed Matthews argues that with the exception of the fourth day, Gen. 8:1–14 parallels Gen. 1–2:3.[12]

> Day 1—The words "earth," "deep," "spirit," "wind" (*ruah*), "waters" are found in both Gen. 1:2 and Gen. 8:1–2.
>
> Day 2—The word "sky," which is in both Gen. 1:7–8 and Gen. 8:2.
>
> Day 3—There is "water and a possible link between the dry ground and the appearance of the mountaintops" in both Gen. 1:9 and Gen. 8:3–5.
>
> Day 4—No mention of the luminaries.
>
> Day 5—There is mention of the birds or the raven being "above the earth" in both Gen. 1:20 and in Gen. 8:7–8.
>
> Day 6—There are the "creatures and the creatures that move along the ground" in both Gen. 1:24 and 8:17.

The observation presented by Matthews is certainly an interesting one. Although it is weak on a number of points, at the very least it demonstrates that the two passages share the same vocabulary and that the story of Noah to some extent seeks to echo Gen. 1–2:3.[13]

Further links between the creation and Noah narratives include mention of man being made in the image of God (Gen. 1:26; 9:6),[14] and the nakedness of Noah which is followed by a curse just as it was for Adam and Eve (Gen. 3:11ff; 9:20ff).[15] In fact, as many have noticed, Noah is presented in the text almost as a second Adam; he is the first to be born after the death of Adam and after Adam he is the next in the *toledot* series,[16] there is the fruitful-

---

12. Matthews, *Genesis 1–11:26*, 383.

13. This is incidentally further evidence against the claim that Gen. 1–2:3 is a later addition to Israel's proto-history.

14. Matthews, *Genesis 1–11:26*, 383.

15. Ibid., 414.

16. Ibid., 36.

ness of the vineyard followed by a fall,[17] God brings the animals to Noah just as he did to Adam in order that they be named,[18] and both are given the commission to fill the earth (Gen. 1:28; 9:7).[19]

Yet at the same time it was not *the* re-creation, Noah and his sons were still sinful, God's judgment is still seen as a future event (Gen. 9:4); God's rest had not come, they had only received relief from the wickedness that had filled the earth before the flood.

It is interesting to note that Noah is commissioned to fill the earth, yet the command to subdue is lacking.[20] This contrasts with Israel's conquest of the land which is spoken of as the land being subdued, which as will be explored later alludes to a type of Edenic restoration. So the absence of the command to subdue the land in Gen. 9:7 emphasizes the point that the flood was not *the* reversal of the fall; man's relationship to creation was still marred by the sin and humanity is still unable to subdue the land as the Lord commanded.[21] The ultimate reversal of the fall in the re-creation was still to come, Noah was not the end of the story, he merely prefigured it.

Reassurance of the Rest to Come

Within the context of contemporary study of Genesis, the argument that the story of Noah functions to prefigure end time events might seem daring. Yet in the wider history of how the story has been used and understood, it is by no means a new idea. One example of this can be seen in Matt. 24:37, where Jesus compares the second coming to the days of Noah. Further still, Jesus' words are spoken into a Jewish context filled with apocryphal writings and Jewish traditions which frame material relating to Noah with an

17. Gage, *The Gospel of Genesis*, 12.

18. Matthews, *Genesis 1–11:26*, 374.

19. Ibid., 400.

20. The translators of the Septuagint chose to add it in to their translation, but its absence from the text has theological import which they did not grasp.

21. Matthews, *Genesis 1–11:26*, 400.

understanding of God's coming judgment. It seemed an obvious thing for many to do, but does the text necessitate such a reading?

The text undeniably presents Noah as a type of Adam and the post-diluvian world as a type of new creation, yet it remains aware of the reality of ongoing sin. How might this tension be otherwise explained? It seems that the text demands an interpretation which takes both the ideological new creation and the reality of a sinful world seriously.

Chapter 3

"Rest" for the Nations

"Rest" was a dominant religious theme not just for the Hebrews, but also within each of the surrounding nations, informing the underlying worldview of the ancient Near East. Once this has been appreciated, the question naturally arising and foremost in the focus of this chapter is: did the Israelites view "rest" differently than the nations, and if so, how?

Rest in the Literature of the Nations

One of the creation stories which emerged from ancient Mesopotamia was the Enuma Elish epic. This myth celebrates the rise of Marduk, the city god of Babylon; the seven tablets which record it date to around 1100BC,[1] yet the origins of the myth likely predate this. Rest is an important concept in the realm of myth and the Enuma Elish epic is perhaps the clearest example to that end.

In this story, the first gods Tiamat, Mother Ocean, and Apsu give birth to a series of other gods. Their offspring however cause such a stir and a clamor that Apsu finds no "rest" and he cannot sleep. As a result Apsu determines to do away with his offspring for the express purpose of having "rest," yet when his children find out about his plan they are stunned to silence. Then the god Ea devises his own plan, he goes to put Apsu to sleep and while he is resting he kills him; having established himself as head of the pantheon

---

1. Just prior to the time of David.

of gods, Ea then rests in his chamber which he calls "Apsu." It is in the midst of this chamber that Marduk is born to Ea and his wife.

In the meantime, the pantheon of gods become angry because they have no "rest" and they beseech Tiamat who is pleased to raise up an army of evil creatures; dragons, serpents, lions and scorpions to war against Ea. Tiamat displaces Ea and in the midst of this tumult, Marduk arises as the champion who in the midst of battle faces a raging Tiamat subduing and killing her. Using Tiamat's carcass Marduk forms the earth, heaven and netherworld and establishes peace amongst the gods. At this point, Marduk decides with Ea to create man in order for them to bear the gods' burden thus allowing the gods to rest. Having divided the gods between the heaven and the netherworld Marduk determines to have his temple and resting place in Babylon.

A number of things should be observed here. Firstly, for the Babylonians, the gods struggle to experience rest and this struggle is symptomatic of humanity's and of nature's own struggle; there is no understanding that the gods are perfect and have no need to struggle as men do, rather they share in the same struggle. Secondly, creation is not from nothing, but is formed out of the chaos of the primeval waters, Tiamat, who is Mother Ocean. This is certainly not unique to the Enuma Elish creation myth; it was widely considered throughout the ancient world that chaos was eternal and from its midst creation came. Third of all, the temple was the place of a particular god's rest, in this case it was Marduk's throne room from which men could also experience rest. This is true even though Marduk's throne and temple are cast primarily in terms of his relationship with the other gods rather than humanity.[2] Lastly there is the point that humanity was thought to exist in order to provide the gods with rest. This does not mean that humanity could not experience rest themselves but rather that they must serve the gods and that in doing so they also could experience this rest.

For a time it was popular to view Gen. 1 as echoing the Enuma Elish epic. Hermann Gunkel put forward the idea that there was a

---

2. Timmer, *Creation, Tabernacle and Sabbath*, 76.

connection between the phrase *tohu wabohu* "formless and void" (Gen. 1:2) and the primordial waters of which Tiamat was god. He supposed there to be suppressed evidence of the idea that the Lord battled Tiamat in establishing his rule upon the earth.[3] This view gave credence to the view dating Gen. 1 as exilic; emerging from a time when the Israelites were exposed to Babylonian myths and put forward Gen. 1 as a polemic. Yet it is now generally recognized that there is no connection between the Hebrew word for "ocean," *tehom,* and the goddess Tiamat, and that the phrase *tohu wabohu* has the sense of emptiness rather than chaos.[4]

The Enuma Elish myth was just one of many which sought to give prominence to a particular local deity. Another creation myth can be found recorded in the Atrahasis epic, commonly dated to the eighteenth century BC.[5] After recording its creation myth, where humanity is similarly created in order to carry the gods' workload, the account proceeds to tell the story of Atrahasis and the flood. In this story, it is when mankind begins to populate the earth that the clamor becomes too great for the gods to bear, so the god Enlil sends a plague to diminish them. Upon hearing this, a man called Atrahasis assembles the elders at the gate and he convinces them not to make reverence, prayer, or sacrifice to the gods but rather make a clamor. Consequently Enlil cannot find rest so he sends a famine to depopulate the earth, which would have been vast but for the help of the god Enki. Frustrated, Enlil plans in the presence of the other gods to send a flood to earth. Enki informs Atrahasis, via a dream, of Enlil's plans and instructs him to build a boat, to accommodate every type of animal and to escape the coming flood.

The Atrahasis epic is not "history" in the same sense that the Genesis account is "history." The Atrahasis epic is concerned with presenting Atrahasis as the hero and functions as political propaganda while simultaneously serving to present a theological

---

3. Gunkel, *Schopfung Und Chaos in Urzeit Und Endzeit.*

4. Tsumura, *Earth and the Waters in Genesis 1 and 2.*

5. Foster, *From Distant Days,* 52.

ideology.[6] Genesis, though perhaps not fitting the contemporary definition for the discipline of "history," is distinct from these mythic forms of propaganda and reports historical events which include the shortcomings of their ancestors, in this case Noah. Moreover the Biblical accounts seek to analyze how past events shape the present which is something mythmakers consistently neglected to do.[7]

In terms of theological differences, in the Atrahasis epic men and gods are always potential enemies. The two struggle to coexist and this struggle is focused on whether the gods have rest. Conversely the writings of the Hebrews present the creator God who possesses rest and whose intention it is for humanity to enjoy this rest together with him.

The final creation account which will be referred to here is the Memphite creation myth. Originating from the city of Memphis, once the capital city of Egypt, Ptah is seen to create order out of chaos.[8] Ptah does this through speaking words and at the end of creation he rests, however the links with Genesis do not extend beyond this. The text cites another Egyptian creation myth, the Heliopolitan creation account where Atum creates by the creative power of his word but asserts that Ptah is older and greater. Acting as a piece of political propaganda, the creation myth suggests that Ptah, the city god of Memphis establishes *"maat"* through the words of his mouth and is justification for Memphis becoming the new capital of Egypt overtaking Hermopolis. Like all the creation myths, creation is ongoing, rest is continually being created out of chaos and as such the myth needs to be continually commemorated.

---

6. Foley, *Companion to Ancient Epic*, 243.

7. Oswalt, *Bible among the Myths*, 49.

8. The dating of Memphite theology is debated, though it was traditionally thought to be at least as old as the Old Kingdom period 2700–2050 BC others such as Ockinga argue for a post-Amarna dating ca. 1300. Ockinga, "Memphite Theology."

In Egyptian thought prior to 1353 and the Amarna period,[9] the land of Egypt was one of order surrounded by chaos, namely the nations which warred against her, famine and disease. The constant threat of chaos though was perceived on the micro- level of the individual as well as the macro- level of the nation; so it could be anything which disturbed the balance of the life of the individual, family or local community. To the Egyptian mind, the way to counter chaos was through the principle of *maat* which ensured harmony through establishing truth and justice and was guaranteed by the ongoing rule of the appointed Pharaoh, who was seen as the guarantor of *maat*.[10]

As with most ancient Near Eastern mythology, creation is the transformation of chaos or primordial waters into cosmos.[11] Rest is a key component of ancient Near Eastern myth because in the idyllic world of myth, chaos is continually being triumphed over and in the place of the chaotic primeval waters, rest is established. For the ancient, the desire was for this mythical world to transcend the visible one and in so doing keep chaos, whether it be social, natural, economic, or political chaos at bay, through ritual and the re-enactment of the myth.[12] As such, it is difficult to overemphasize just how pervasive the theme of rest is with ancient Near Eastern worldviews.

Conflicting Worldviews

Unlike Israel, the surrounding nations functioned within what John Oswalt calls a "mythic" worldview; one which sees essential continuity in the relationship between deity, humanity, and nature.[13] Some of the unique features of this worldview include: an

9. The Amarna period was a short period in Egyptian history in which the Pharaoh attempted to change the make-up of Egyptian society and religion.

10. Assmann, *The Mind of Egypt*, 109.

11. Hasenfratz, "Patterns of Creation in Ancient Egypt," 176.

12. Oswalt, *The Bible among the Myths*, 42.

13. Ibid.

emphasis on the cyclical nature of time, an obsession with fertility and the need for ongoing re-creation and a denial of boundaries which serve to emphasize the oneness and continuity which exists between deity, humanity, and nature, for instance sexual boundaries which entailed the acceptability of incest and bestiality. They also tend to hold to a low view of the gods who can make mistakes, a low view of humanity where humans have no control over their destinies because they are insignificant and the purely social function of ethics which have the sole purpose of ensuring order.

In contrast the solitary existence of Israel's markedly different worldview, which if not attributed to prior reception of divine revelation, cannot easily be explained as a natural sociological phenomenon, stands in sharp contrast to the worldview of the surrounding nations. For the Hebrews time was not primarily cyclical but linear, and as a consequence an interest in the past and in historical events is far more important to the Israelites than to her neighbors. God is distinct from his creation and is sovereign over it such that its existence relies purely and solely on him who is perfect and righteous in all of his ways. Humans relate to God both communally and individually and adherence to law is envisioned as an act of worship where the moral boundaries are conditioned by a good and holy God.

This analysis leads Oswalt to conclude that the similarities between Israel and the nations are merely "superficial" in comparison to the differences which are "essential."[14] This is a worthy evaluation which should undergird any study which contrasts the theology of the nations with that of the Israelites. Regardless of any similarities that can be observed, there are fundamental differences. In the case of rest, for the nations, it is the outcome of the gods' conflict with chaos, whereas for Israel rest is the result of living in accordance with God's word.

The point being made, of time being primarily linear in Israel's faith is very significant. Both the start and the end are framed by the rest which God gives. It is not earned or established through the actions of human beings, as it is in the worldview of the other

14. Ibid., 47.

nations. Rather it is freely given by him, who is sovereign over all. Within the Old Testament, any chaos or restlessness that exists does so because it is God's judgment on sin, not as an opposing force against which the Lord fights. Indeed "chaos" is the wrong word, because it is not outside of God's control; God has chosen to allow the fallen state of humanity to continue for a time, desiring that humanity turn to back him.

A Message for the Nations?

Israel's understanding of "rest" had a missional dimension to it, in that it was possible for non-Israelites to experience it if they turned away from their idolatry and alternative worldviews to rely upon the grace of God; examples of which will be observed in the course of this study. The message Israel had for the nations included an open invitation for anyone to enjoy God's rest through submission to his word and by entering into covenant with him. In such a worldview ritual did not ensure rest through warring against chaos, rather it provided a limited experience of rest in the present and it was a prefiguring of the consummation of the rest still to come. Note for example in the case of Sabbath which will be attended to in the next chapter, the invitation is open for all to experience this rest.

There are a couple of questions that need to be answered though in order to substantiate this claim. First of all, to what degree does the Old Testament engage with and respond to the belief systems of the surrounding nations? Secondly, is an eschatological reading of the Old Testament valid?

In responding to the question as to how Israel engages with the worldview of her neighbors, it is important to recognize that she was aware of what they believed. Not only was there active trade and communication between the nations of the Middle East but of course the Israelites had themselves once come from Egypt. How well read the Israelites were with regard to the literature of the nations prior to the conquest, is not hugely important. It is entirely possible to imagine an environment where Israel knew the gist of what various nations believed without having read their literature, much in the same way that people today can know the gist of Darwin's "origin of the species" without having read it for themselves.[15] Israel's message is unique, not because it does not belong to the world, nor because they were incapable of relating their beliefs to the world. Rather it is unique because at the same time as using concepts and forms familiar to the world, it projected a message diametrically opposed to the worldviews of the surrounding nations.[16]

Is an eschatological reading of the Pentateuch valid? Many contemporary scholars consider the thought of an eschaton to be a late idea, even viewing the Pentateuch as being "anti-eschatological."[17] Further still there are others who have recognized eschatological thought in the Pentateuch yet maintained that eschatology is a late idea which the Israelites redacted in, for it is held that there is evidence that early Israelites did not believe in an afterlife.[18]

Certainly there are passages which suggest the loss of hope after death (e.g. Ps. 6:5; 30:9; 88:10–12; Job 10:21–22; Is. 38:18), but the context in all of these passages is best understood as an individual facing the prospect of death under God's wrath and without the forgiveness of sin.[19] Moreover there are clear instances of the righteous enjoying life with God even after death, for instance Ps. 23:6.

In turning to think upon the beliefs and worldviews of Israel's neighbors, it should be noted that all of them held a belief in the after-life.[20] So one would expect this notion, of there being no life after death, to be a central and distinctive feature of Israel's faith.

---

15. Wenham, "The Perplexing Pentateuch," 12.

16. Oswalt, *The Bible among the Myths*, 103.

17. Crusemann, *The Torah: Theology and Social History of Old Testament Law*, 346.

18. Ploger, *Theocracy and Eschatology*.

19. Motyer, *The Prophecy of Isaiah*, 295.

20. Spronk, *Beatific Afterlife in Ancient Israel and in the Ancient Near East*.

Yet the opposite is true, the distinctive nature of Israel's belief is rather to be found in a coming judgment and re-creation, where God's eternal rest is restored.

Chapter 4

Sabbath Rest

Israel's Sabbath rest is a distinctive feature of Israelite faith and underlines the distinctiveness of Israel's theology of rest rooted as it was in their understanding of how the world came to be. This chapter reinforces a number of points that have been made already; that Israel's understanding of rest was a message for the nations and that Israel's expectation was of a re-creation and restoration of Eden.

Genesis in the Ten Commandments

> Remember the sabbath day, to keep it holy. Six days you shall labor and do all your work, but the seventh day is a sabbath of the Lord your God; in it you shall not do any work, you or your son or your daughter, your male or your female servant or your cattle or your sojourner who stays with you. For in six days the Lord made the heavens and the earth, the sea and all that is in them, and rested on the seventh day; therefore the Lord blessed the sabbath day and made it holy.
>
> Exodus 20:8–11

The sabbatical ceasing (*sbt*) is intimately connected to concept of rest (*nuah*) and this is made explicit here in verse 11; because whereas Gen. 2:3 states that God ceased, here the verb *nuah* is used.

The book of Exodus assumes that Sabbath observance was already practiced, so the commandment here is not the institution of something new; the story of the Israelites collecting manna in the desert (Ex.16) implies that the Sabbath was already in existence before Sinai.

Perhaps even more significant than this though, is that both Ex. 16 and Ex.20 assume an awareness of Gen. 1—2:3. In the past it was suggested that the different verbs being used was evidence that Ex. 20:11 was not dependent on Gen. 2:1–3.[1] Yet the only way to maintain such a view is to argue that the texts concerning the Ten Commandments were significantly edited; which would require the editor to have an attitude to God's law foreign to the one being propounded in the Old Testament itself. Moreover there would need to be an alternative suggestion for the origins of the Sabbath. As documented below though, this is something that scholars have failed to do.

For these reasons, an early date for the origin of the Sabbath will be assumed just as the text intimates; being founded at the very least on an oral tradition very close to Gen. 1—2:3.

The Uniqueness of Israel's Sabbath

For a time it was widely thought that Israel's Sabbath had its roots in the customs of either Canaanite New Moon festivals or Babylonian traditions, to which the Israelites became properly exposed to at the time of the exile.

In the Akkadian calendar, *shappattu* was the middle day of the month, a day which supposedly formed a partial basis for the Israelite custom.[2] This then was then synthesized into another Babylonian custom; where the 7th, 14th, 19th, 21st, and 28th days of a month are designated "evil" by certain Babylonian texts. These days were unsuitable for desirable action and people were

1. Robinson, *The Origin and Development of the Old Testament Sabbath: A Comprehensive Exegetical Approach*, 227.

2. Cassuto, *From Adam to Noah: A Commentary on the Book of Genesis, Part 1*, 64.

restricted in what they could do; for instance the priest could not deliver oracles, the physician could not touch the sick and the king could not eat cooked meat, change his clothes or go out in his chariot.[3]

This view and others like it have been largely abandoned following an article by the respected Assyriologist William Hallo, who debunked the theory of Mesopotamian origins of the Sabbath, for the reasons that the Babylonians organized their lives by months not weeks and that the Sabbath is too deeply woven into the Pentateuch for it to be possible.[4]

The consensus following Hallo's critique has been almost unanimous recognition of the uniqueness of Israel's Sabbath, which was an entirely foreign practice to the surrounding nations and built upon a fundamentally different cosmogony. This is certainly true; the surrounding nations held creation myths which were theogonies, stories about the creation of the gods, whereas the Genesis account presents a story of how the world came be, structured around the seven day Sabbath concept.[5]

The Eschatological Overtones of the Sabbath

It has already been noted in the chapter on creation that God's resting in Gen. 2 holds in the background an understanding of a coming re-creation and resulting eternal rest. Yet this interpretation is further sanctioned upon looking at the Israelites' cultic calendar.

In addition to the Sabbath, the Pentateuch outlines seven festivals which the Israelites must observe; Passover, the Feast of Unleavened Bread, the Feast of the Firstfruits, the Feast of Weeks which take place near the beginning of the year, and then the Feast of Trumpets, the Day of Atonement and the Feast of Tabernacles, which take place within the seventh month, the month of Tishri.

---

3. De Vaux, *Ancient Israel: Its Life and Institutions*, 476.
4. Hallo, "New Moons and Sabbaths."
5. Currid, *Ancient Egypt in the Old Testament*, 72.

All of these festivals in some way relate to concept of "rest" and are holy conventions (*miqra*), that is, a call to worship and connected to the reading of Scripture.[6] For instance there is the reading of the law in Nehemiah 8 and 9, for the Feast of Trumpets and the Feast of Tabernacles respectively.

On this point, special note should be given to the Feast of Tabernacles, which in some senses summarizes and refers to all the other feasts.[7] It was the seventh feast which coincided with the end of harvest time and was a time of great joy. The first and eighth days were prescribed as Sabbath rests and the seventh Feast of Tabernacles is given special mention by Moses in particular:

> So Moses wrote this law and gave it to the priests, the sons of Levi who carried the ark of the covenant of the Lord, and to all the elders of Israel. Then Moses commanded them, saying, "At the end of *every* seven years, at the time of the year of remission of debts, at the Feast of Booths, when all Israel comes to appear before the Lord your God at the place which He will choose, you shall read this law in front of all Israel in their hearing. Assemble the people, the men and the women and children and the alien who is in your town, so that they may hear and learn and fear the Lord your God, and be careful to observe all the words of this law. Their children, who have not known, will hear and learn to fear the Lord your God, as long as you live on the land which you are about to cross the Jordan to possess."
>
> Deuteronomy 31:9–13

This text will be referred to later as well when looking at the consecration of the temple, but the eschatological overtones to this festival should not be missed. In celebrating the Feast of Tabernacles the Israelites were anticipating the eternal rest to come. In fact this is the only time for which Israelites are commanded to rejoice in the Lord.[8] At such a time, the word of God takes center

---

6. Wenham, *Book of Leviticus*, 301.

7. Kiuchi, *Leviticus*, 427.

8. Rooker, *Leviticus*, 290.

stage because it is the assurance of the rest to come and the means by which they would experience it. This point is further evidenced in other texts for example Zech. 14:16–21, which aligns the feast with the day of the Lord.[9]

The Sabbath principle informs all of the Pentateuchal festivals; there are seven festivals each year and contained within them are seven days of rest, the first and seventh of the Feast of Unleavened Bread, the Feast of Weeks, the Feast of Trumpets, the Day of Atonement and the first and last days of the Feast of Tabernacles.[10]

Indeed the Sabbath principle influences the jubilee regulations which were to take place at the passing of every seven Sabbath years. Even though Scripture itself makes clear that the Sabbath was not observed, its ideological significance should not be downplayed, it was the sign of the covenant (Ex. 31) and it was not even set aside for the construction of the tabernacle (Ex. 35), such was its importance and sanctity.[11]

Mission and the Sabbath Day

The Sabbath is God's day just as it is his rest. The idea that "rest" is something which belongs to God is made explicit for example in Ps. 95:11, "they shall not enter into My rest," yet it is assumed even from the creation account. The Sabbath is made holy by God and so they are rightfully *his* Sabbaths (e.g. Neh. 9:14, Is. 58:13, Eze. 22:8).

That the sojourner dwelling amongst the Israelites must also observe the Sabbath (Ex. 20:10), is a clear sign that the Sabbath is not meant to be exclusive. Though it is one of the distinctive features of Israel's worship, non-Israelites are encouraged and invited to experience God's rest for themselves. This is no small point; in the ancient world strangers were normally beyond the protection of the law.[12] The fact then that Israel's law includes them

9. Schaefer, "Ending of the Book of Zechariah."

10. Keil, *Manual of Biblical Archaeology*, 1:469.

11. Jacob, *Second Book of the Bible*, 847.

12. Sarna, *Exodus*, 113.

in this, speaks volumes not only about the kindness required of the Israelite towards the foreigner but also the greatness and love of the God they served. Certainly there were occasions when the foreigner was excluded, for example the Passover meal, yet the invitation to experience the Lord's rest was an open one.

The missional nature of the Sabbath is further spelled out in Isaiah 56:

> Thus says the Lord,
> "Preserve justice and do righteousness,
> For My salvation is about to come
> And My righteousness to be revealed.
> How blessed is the man who does this,
> And the son of man who takes hold of it;
> Who keeps from profaning the sabbath,
> And keeps his hand from doing any evil."
> Let not the foreigner who has joined himself to the Lord say,
> "The Lord will surely separate me from His people."
> Nor let the eunuch say, "Behold, I am a dry tree."
> For thus says the Lord,
> "To the eunuchs who keep My sabbaths,
> And choose what pleases Me,
> And hold fast My covenant,
> To them I will give in My house and within My walls a memorial,
> And a name better than that of sons and daughters;
> I will give them an everlasting name which will not be cut off.
> Also the foreigners who join themselves to the Lord,
> To minister to Him, and to love the name of the Lord,
> To be His servants, every one who keeps from profaning the sabbath
> And holds fast My covenant;

Even those I will bring to My holy mountain

And make them joyful in My house of prayer.

Their burnt offerings and their sacrifices will be acceptable on My altar;

For My house will be called a house of prayer for all the peoples."

The Lord God, who gathers the dispersed of Israel, declares,

"Yet *others* I will gather to them, to those *already* gathered."

Isaiah 56:1–8

The first thing that should be mentioned regarding the focus on Sabbath observance in the last chapters of Isaiah, is that Isaiah is not promoting a ritualistic, religious Sabbath observance which qualifies someone to be included within the people of God. This becomes obvious when it is remembered that Is. 1:13 explicitly criticizes such Sabbath keeping.

Having just presented an invitation of grace in chapter 55, for the thirsty to come and those without money to come and eat, it would be ridiculous to interpret Is. 56 to say that a foreigner could earn salvation through Sabbath observance.

The role of the Sabbath in these chapters has been used as an argument for dating Is. 56–66 as post exilic. Supposedly the exile was a time when many forms of Israel's worship had been brought to an end and so the theory goes, Sabbath observance took on more importance as an expression of faith.[13] The reality however is that there is no evidence firstly to suggest that the Israelites had the freedom to continue to observe the Sabbath while in Babylon and secondly it overlooks the fact that ill observance of the Sabbath was a very real pre-exilic problem (see for example Amos 8:5, Eze. 20:12–13 and Is. 1:13).[14]

Why then should the Sabbath be given such attention? Firstly it is important to recognize that Sabbath observance and holding

13. De Vaux, *Ancient Israel: Its Life and Institutions*, 476.

14. Motyer, *The Prophecy of Isaiah*, 465.

fast to God's covenant come hand in hand (Is. 56:6) because the Sabbath is a sign of the covenant. Secondly, Sabbath observance was such a unique feature of Israelite worship which was not held by other nations, that by observing the Sabbath the foreigner makes such an overt commitment to the Lord, rejecting the pattern of the other nations and looking to God as creator and omnipotent.[15] This entails turning one's back on a belief that rest could be earned or ensured through ritual and believing upon the Almighty God who alone graciously grants rest.

15. Ibid.

Chapter 5

The Tabernacle

There is certainly a rich base of imagery connecting Eden, the tabernacle, and the temple. Yet, each deserves their own separate treatment, namely because the theology concerning temple construction is not anachronistically transposed onto the Exodus accounts of tabernacle construction, nor is Gen. 1 merely a reflection of priestly thought where God's creation is temple like.

While there are indeed echoes of Gen. 1–3 in the accounts of tabernacle construction, it is by no means clear that the reverse is true. Despite the majority of scholars arguing otherwise, Gen. 1–3 never explicitly presents creation as a temple nor is it necessarily implied; the common language shared by both the creation, tabernacle and temple accounts, do not necessitate a reading where Genesis intentionally presents Eden as a temple.[1] As has already been observed, Gen. 1 ordinances the Sabbath, which as the book of Exodus makes clear was being practiced before Moses was given instructions regarding the tabernacle. Though the creation myths of the nations often involve the creation of a temple for the god to live in, it is hard to argue that God created Eden in order to provide a home for himself.[2]

Similarly, suggestions that the tabernacle construction in Exodus reflect the later construction of the temple also fail in the light of evidence. Though there are undoubtedly parallels between

1. Block, "Eden: A Temple?"
2. Ibid., 24.

the accounts of both temple and tabernacle construction, the construction of the tabernacle provided the template for the temple rather than the reverse.

The evidence for dismountable tabernacles date as far back as the third millennium with the tomb of Queen Hetepheres at Giza.[3] It is not just in Egypt though, tabernacles have also been found from the kingdom of Mari in modern day Syria, where the wooden frames for transporting the tabernacle are named *qersu'* which is similar to the Hebrew term *qershim*,[4] and also in north-eastern Sinai, where a Middianite tabernacle was found.[5] This is in contrast to the absence of evidence for tabernacles among the Assyrians and Babylonians.[6] The most significant piece of evidence though is that Tuthmosis III (ca 1479–1425BC) is known to have built a temple which was a translation into stone of a pillared tent.[7] This provides a strong basis not only for thinking that the tabernacle was a historical reality, but also that the vision of one day building a temple in the likeness of the tabernacle had its origins in the time of the Exodus.

Tabernacle and Re-creation

There are numerous links between the tabernacle construction and Gen. 1–3: the cherubim who guard both Eden and the Ark of the Covenant; the menorah which is often recognized as being symbolic of the tree of life;[8] the spirit of the Lord which fills Bezalel (Ex. 31:3) and is present in the process of creation;[9] the fact that the priests were commanded to keep and serve the sanctuary just as God commanded Adam (Gen. 2:15);[10] and that Moses sees and

---

3. Kitchen, *On the Reliability of the Old Testament*, 276.

4. Fleming, "Mari's Large Public Tent and the Priestly Tent Sanctuary."

5. Rothenberg, *Timna: Valley of the Biblical Copper Mines*.

6. Kitchen, *On the Reliability of the Old Testament*, 277.

7. Ibid., 278.

8. Wenham, "Sanctuary Symbolism in the Garden of Eden Story," 402.

9. Fishbane, *Biblical Text and Texture*, 12.

10. Wenham, *Genesis 1–15*, 67.

evaluates the work of the tabernacle (Ex. 31:1) just as God sees and evaluates creation.[11] In addition to this, there are the seven days of creation, which are mirrored by the seven speeches which God makes (Ex. 25:1–30; 30:11–16; 30:17–21; 30:22–33; 30:34–38; 31:1–11; 31:12–17),[12] and the placement of the Sabbath which concludes both the six days and the six sections of tabernacle construction, where the Sabbath is marked as a sign of the covenant.[13]

These echoes of the creation narrative here in Exodus carry theological significance; the tabernacle and the temple which it anticipated were symbols of the rest which would one day come. Just as the tabernacle was erected on the first day of the year (Ex.40:2), so the Israelites looked ahead to a new start and restoration of Eden where God dwelt among men. Hence the tabernacle is "patterned" on God's heavenly sanctuary and is symbolic of his presence with them (Ex. 25:9).

Tabernacle and Rest

Although there is attention given to the Sabbath day in Ex. 31, there is little explicit mention of rest, which contrasts with the temple construction as recorded in Kings. The reason for this is that the tabernacle is a temporary feature during Israel's wanderings, prior to erection of the temple which is the Lord's resting place in the land; as such the tabernacle is primarily concerned with rest in that it points forward to the future resting place. This is most clearly seen in Moses' song, in Ex.15.

The song of the Sea is widely considered to have early origins, given its use of archaic Hebrew.[14] The song praises God for saving the Israelites from under the Egyptians and bringing them to the mountain of the LORD.

---

11. Frethaim, *Exodus*, 271.
12. Kearney, "Creation and Liturgy," 375.
13. Blenkinsopp, "The Structure of P." 281.
14. Hoffmeier, *Israel in Egypt*, 201.

Then Moses and the sons of Israel sang this song to the Lord, and said,

"I will sing to the Lord, for He is highly exalted;

The horse and its rider He has hurled into the sea.

The Lord is my strength and song,

And He has become my salvation;

This is my God, and I will praise Him;

My father's God, and I will extol Him.

The Lord is a warrior;

The Lord is His name.

Pharaoh's chariots and his army He has cast into the sea;

And the choicest of his officers are drowned in the Red Sea.

The deeps cover them;

They went down into the depths like a stone.

Your right hand, O Lord, is majestic in power,

Your right hand, O Lord, shatters the enemy.

And in the greatness of Your excellence You overthrow those who rise up against You;

You send forth Your burning anger, and it consumes them as chaff.

At the blast of Your nostrils the waters were piled up,

The flowing waters stood up like a heap;

The deeps were congealed in the heart of the sea.

The enemy said, 'I will pursue, I will overtake, I will divide the spoil;

My desire shall be gratified against them;

I will draw out my sword, my hand will destroy them.'

You blew with Your wind, the sea covered them;

They sank like lead in the mighty waters.

Who is like You among the gods, O Lord?

Who is like You, majestic in holiness,

Awesome in praises, working wonders?

> You stretched out Your right hand,
>
> The earth swallowed them.
>
> In Your lovingkindness You have led the people whom You
> have redeemed;
>
> In Your strength You have guided them to Your holy
> habitation.
>
> The peoples have heard, they tremble;
>
> Anguish has gripped the inhabitants of Philistia.
>
> Then the chiefs of Edom were dismayed;
>
> The leaders of Moab, trembling grips them;
>
> All the inhabitants of Canaan have melted away.
>
> Terror and dread fall upon them;
>
> By the greatness of Your arm they are motionless as stone;
>
> Until Your people pass over, O Lord,
>
> Until the people pass over whom You have purchased.
>
> You will bring them and plant them in the mountain of Your
> inheritance,
>
> The place, O Lord, which You have made for Your dwelling,
>
> The sanctuary, O Lord, which Your hands have established.
>
> The Lord shall reign forever and ever."

Exodus 15:1–18

The song pictures God leading his people who he has redeemed from
Egypt into the land, which culminates at the end of the song with
Israel coming to worship God on "the mountain of his inheritance."
This is a strange phrase occurring nowhere else in the canon, yet it
is found in the Ugaritic literature where it refers to Mount Zaphon,
the sanctuary of Baal.[15] Baal, the Canaanite storm God had a temple
on Mount Zaphon where he reigned having overcome his enemies.
Canaanites worshipped him there, giving thanks also for the waters
which came from the mountain and brought forth the harvests.[16]
The song paints a picture of the Lord defeating Baal and establishing

15. Sarna, *Exodus*, 82.
16. Clifford, *Cosmic Mountain*, 191.

his everlasting rule in his stead; it will become the mountain of the Lord's inheritance and his resting place. While this song certainly contained a hope held by the Israelites, it also contained a message for the nations which would have been readily understandable to them. As made clear in the song, the nations would hear and tremble at what the Lord was doing amongst them.

The Tabernacle and God's Word

The tabernacle of course housed the Ark of the Covenant which contained the Ten Commandments. Here the interplay between God's rest, his word, and his presence come into focus, where it becomes difficult to speak of the one without the other; God's presence is concurrent with God's rest (Ex. 33:14) and both are experienced and promised through obedience to God's word. It is only through keeping God's word that an individual can encounter God and it is only through the power of God's word that his rest will be enjoyed and established.

Indeed the structure of the tabernacle mirrors Mount Sinai in their division of three zones; the summit, partway up the mountain, and the foot of the mountain which correspond to the holy of holies, outer sanctum, and outer court.[17] Similarly just as the cloud descends on Sinai, so it descends on the tabernacle.[18] The tabernacle thereby functions as a kind of "movable Sinai,"[19] which after Sinai, goes ahead of the Israelites to find them a place to "rest" (Num. 10:33–36).

17. Averbeck, "Tabernacle," 812.

18. Blackburn, *God Who Makes Himself Known*, 131.

19. Averbeck, "Tabernacle," 824.

Chapter 6

The Land as an Inheritance

The introduction put forward the case for including the concept of "inheritance" (*nahalah*) within this study of rest (*nuah*), both because it shares a linguistic root and because it is so closely associated conceptually within Scripture. This is most evidently seen in Deut. 12:8–12 and Deut. 25:17–19, which are given close examination in this chapter.

Deuteronomy 12

> You shall not do at all what we are doing here today, every man doing whatever is right in his own eyes; for you have not as yet come to the resting place and the inheritance which the Lord your God is giving you. When you cross the Jordan and live in the land which the Lord your God is giving you to inherit, and He gives you rest from all your enemies around you so that you live in security, then it shall come about that the place in which the Lord your God will choose for His name to dwell, there you shall bring all that I command you: your burnt offerings and your sacrifices, your tithes and the contribution of your hand, and all your choice votive offerings which you will vow to the Lord. And you shall rejoice before the Lord your God, you and your sons and daughters, your male and female servants, and the Levite who is within your gates, since he has no portion or inheritance with you.
>
> Deuteronomy 12:8–12

Chapter 12 begins a new section in Deuteronomy; following on from chapters 5–11 which outlined the general stipulations of the covenant treaty, chapter 12 begins a section detailing these stipulations, in a pattern loosely governed by the structure of the Ten Commandments.[1] Specifically Deut. 12:8–12 details some of the implications of what "having no gods before me" looks like.

Modern critical scholarship, beginning with Wilhelm de Wette, took the view that this text must be a later addition, on the grounds that the text intimates Jerusalem and the temple as the central sanctuary and therefore likely originated with Josiah's centralizing of worship in Jerusalem.[2] Indeed this led to it being a commonly held belief that the whole book of Deuteronomy is the product of later period in Israel's history. Yet there are a number of problems with this view; to begin with Jerusalem and the temple were at the heart of Josiah's reforms but neither is mentioned explicitly, and the phrase "from among the tribes" would not likely have originated from the time of Josiah, because the tribal divisions had ceased four hundred years before Josiah came to the throne.[3] Moreover such a view does not benefit from the understanding arrived at during the latter half of the twentieth century, that Deuteronomy takes the shape of an ancient Near Eastern suzerain-vassal treaty commonly found in the late Bronze Age.[4] Within such a structure Deut. 12 is by no means an insignificant text, which might possibly have been inserted at a later date; typically within a vassal treaty the great king resides in a palace in the central city to which the client princes and peoples must come periodically to present their tributes, as stipulated in the treaty.[5]

This analysis corroborates what was postulated in the previous chapter; in the mind of the Hebrews during the wilderness, the

1. Wright, *Deuteronomy*, 158.

2. Merrill, "Deuteronomy and de Wette: A Fresh Look at a Fallacious Premise."

3. Bakon, "Centralization of Worship," 31.

4. This makes it hard not to ascribe an early date for at least the bulk of the Deuteronomy.

5. Merrill, *Deuteronomy*, 221.

tabernacle was only a foreshadowing of a temple which was to be built at a time when the land had been subdued.

On this point, it is clear from within the passage that their experience of life in the desert did not provide a paradigm for life when settled in the Promised Land: "you shall not do at all you we are doing here today, every man doing whatever is right in his own eyes." The distinguishing factor being that while they are living in the desert they do not have God's rest, yet the land will be a resting place for them.[6]

Note that the formulas "rest from your enemies around" and "a place for his name to dwell," found in this text will continue to come up throughout the course of this study; as the biblical narrative works out the implications of God's command and promise through history.

Deuteronomy 25

> Remember what Amalek did to you along the way when you came out from Egypt, how he met you along the way and attacked among you all the stragglers at your rear when you were faint and weary; and he did not fear God. Therefore it shall come about when the Lord your God has given you rest from all your surrounding enemies, in the land which the Lord your God gives you as an inheritance to possess, you shall blot out the memory of Amalek from under heaven; you must not forget.
>
> Deuteronomy 25:17–19

The text here forms an inclusio with the passage cited above from Deut. 12, bracketing this central section in Deuteronomy, which expounds the stipulations of Israel's covenant in detail.[7] Once again it is possible to observe a connection between God's word and his rest; God's commands to the Israelites are framed by his promise of rest which in one sense is given freely and guaranteed

---

6. Craigie, *The Book of Deuteronomy*, 218.

7. McConville, *Deuteronomy*, 373.

simply by the fact that the Lord spoke it, yet at the same time, are in some way conditioned by their obedience to his commands.

The final chapters of this middle section (Deut. 23–26) have as their central theme care and compassion for the poor and the weak, which loosely correlate to the commandment against covetousness. A note on the coming judgment on the Amalekites is fitting in this context because of the lack of compassion which the Amalekites had for the Israelites in their wilderness wanderings.[8]

The extermination of the Amalekites did not take place during the conquest of the land and this notable failure is embodied by Saul's disobedience when he spared King Agag (1 Sam. 15). This later surfaces in the book of Esther when Haman the Agagite persecutes the Jews and the subject is also dealt with again in the genealogies of Chronicles (1 Chr. 4:13). The theme of rest remains prominent for the writers in the recording of these events, and shall be traced in further detail during the course of this study.[9]

The Land as Inheritance

What does it mean to call the land an "inheritance?" Certainly it alludes to the idea of it being given not only for the Israelites but also for their children's children, and possibly it includes the idea of them being adopted as sons of God.[10] Yet might it not also signify having a share in the world to come, even as the temple signified the Lord's heavenly abode? It is important for example to consider the fact that the Levites would not inherit any land because the Lord himself would be their inheritance (Deut. 10:9), a phrase implying that their communion with God would be maintained even in the

---

8. Block, *Deuteronomy*, 292.

9. A possible word play also exists in the telling also of the Israelites defeat of the Amalekites under the leadership of Moses and Joshua (Ex. 17:8ff). Here the Israelites find success when Moses arms are raised to God, yet not when they are lowered the Israelites begin to lose, so Moses rests (*nuah*) his arms on stones. In this passage also God promises to blot out the Amalekites (Ex. 17:14).

10. VanGemeren, "'Abba' in the Old Testament?"

face of death.[11] Weinfeld in his study finds reason for such a view, pointing for example to Is. 57:13, "he who takes refuge in Me will inherit the land and will possess My holy mountain," yet argues that this idea is a "second temple spiritualization of the land."[12]

Putting to one side Weinfeld's dating of Isaiah, one does not have to search only in the second temple literature in order to find such spiritualizations. In Psalm 27 for instance, David imagines his life as a wandering through the desert together with the tabernacle yet longing to worship God in his temple, in the land of the living.

> One thing I have asked from the Lord, that I shall seek:
>
> That I may dwell in the house of the Lord all the days of my life,
>
> To behold the beauty of the Lord
>
> And to meditate in His temple.
>
> For in the day of trouble He will conceal me in His tabernacle;
>
> In the secret place of His tent He will hide me;
>
> He will lift me up on a rock.
>
> And now my head will be lifted up above my enemies around me,
>
> And I will offer in His tent sacrifices with shouts of joy;
>
> I will sing, yes, I will sing praises to the Lord.
>
> I would have despaired unless I had believed that I would see the goodness of the Lord
>
> In the land of the living.
>
> Wait for the Lord;
>
> Be strong and let your heart take courage;
>
> Yes, wait for the Lord.
>
> Psalm 27:4–8, 13–14

Of course David was already living in the land, yet in this Psalm the land is spiritualized to refer to a heavenly abode. Even still

11. von Rad, *Old Testament Theology*, 1:404.

12. Weinfeld, *The Promise of the Land*.

Weinfeld's comment above raises an interesting question; did the ancient Israelites on the verge of entering the land, also operate with such eschatological vision?

For von Rad this idea was inconceivable; while he understood the Chronicler's theology of rest to be "eschatological," as far as he was concerned Deuteronomy contained no "eschatological vision."[13] It is not possible to fully respond to this view here because the theme of "rest" in the chronicler is still to be examined. Indeed it would be better to see the entirety of this project as a response to von Rad's multiple theologies of "rest" approach; the hypothesis being defended here is that there is one coherent theology of rest, which transcends the books of Deuteronomy and Chronicles amongst others. As such it is not unimportant for this study to show that the ancient Hebrews entering Canaan also spiritualized the conquest of the land. Otherwise the only alternative explanation would be that later generations took up their father's vain hopes of a rest fulfilled by the land and spiritualized them in order to adapt the religion to the reality of their experience of life in the land.

While it is true that the land is at times painted with "paradisiacal imagery,"[14] for instance Deut. 11:10 which reads: "the land, into which you are entering to possess it, is not like the land of Egypt from which you came, where you used to sow your seed and water it with your foot like a vegetable garden." Deuteronomy plainly lays out its laws with an awareness that the Israelites will continue to struggle with sin. For example Deut. 22:13ff which outlines the laws occasioning various forms of adultery. It is a land which at one level is imagined as being Edenic, a land flowing with milk and honey, and yet simultaneously a sin stained land.

The only conceivable way of recognizing this tension and at the same time maintaining the unity of the book of Deuteronomy with its early date, is to accept that the paradisiacal portrayal of the land represents a theological reflection on the conquest of the land. This conjecture will only be further evidenced in the next

13. von Rad, *The Problem of the Hexateuch and Other Essays*, 95–97.

14. von Rad, *Deuteronomy*, 92.

chapter, upon looking at the understanding of rest in the book of Joshua. This is because in Joshua, the land of Canaan is even more explicitly painted with an Edenic brush, even though it retains an awareness of the shortcomings of the conquest and of the Israelites.

Chapter 7

Rest in the Book of Joshua

The land is not Joshua's prominent theme, into which rest is used merely as a metaphor. Rather it is the theology of rest which governs how the land and its conquest are portrayed within the book. This is seen right from the beginning where Joshua says to the Transjordan tribes in Josh. 1:13, "remember the word which Moses the servant of the Lord commanded you, saying, 'the Lord your God gives you rest and will give you this land.'" The "rest" here is not so much rest from warring with enemies (*shaqat*), because the verb *nuah* is used. Moreover, God giving rest precedes the giving of the land, making it unlikely. Rather it appears that rest is the prominent theme.

Rest in the Book of Joshua

The proposed connection between God's word and his rest is clearly demonstrated within the book of Joshua. This point is underlined in the concluding verses of one of the major sections of Joshua, Josh. 13–21, which lays out the apportioning of each tribe's inheritance:

> So the Lord gave Israel all the land which He had sworn to give to their fathers, and they possessed it and lived in it. And the Lord gave them rest on every side, according to all that He had sworn to their fathers, and no one of all their enemies stood before them; the Lord gave all their

> enemies into their hand. Not one of the good promises
> which the Lord had made to the house of Israel failed; all
> came to pass.

Joshua 21:43–45

The idea of rest as the cessation of war is common here and throughout the book (Josh. 11:23; 14:15; 22:4; 23:1). In addition to this of course is the idea of the land being an inheritance which although present in the first half of the book (Josh. 11:23), becomes the central focus in the second part, the division of the land as the inheritance of the various tribes. The texts which the author of Joshua has in mind would seem to be Num. 32:20–22, Deut. 3:18–20 and 12:8–12, echoing these passages and making it explicitly clear that all these events took place in fulfillment of what God had spoken.

The continuity in thought between the Pentateuch and the book of Joshua on the subject of "rest" is no small incident considering the changes that took place between the writing of the Pentateuch and the writing of Joshua. Most probably, the book of Joshua should be dated to a time just preceding David's rise to the throne.[1] This assertion assumes the unity of Joshua and rightly so; the book shows clear signs of being structured, the first and last chapters frame the text with a hortatory tone and there are cases of it being self referencing, for instance the echo of Josh. 1:12 in Josh. 22:1.[2]

---

1. Note that it is possible to put some kind of date to the book of Joshua because of the repeated "to this day" references. For example Josh. 15:63 talks about the Jebusites living in Jerusalem "to this day." Yet David expelled the Jebusites from Jerusalem (2 Sam. 5:6–10), so a date for the writing of Joshua is needed before the rule of David at the latest. Certainly some time would had to have passed for the use of "to this day" to be appropriate, so even when it says that Rahab lives to this day (Josh. 6:25) it likely means her descendants (Pitkanen, *Joshua*, 160). While source critics tried to assign the majority of the text to an exilic date, this would make little sense of the text as a Canaanite polemic, because the Canaanites cease to appear in the historical writings after 1 Kgs. 9. Hess, *Joshua*, 37.

2. Woudstra, *Book of Joshua*, 15.

In spite of Israel's unfaithfulness during the time of the Judges and the gradual descent into idolatry, the preservation of Israel's theology of rest by supposedly a minority of faithful Israelites, not tainted by the theologies of the other people groups, is quite remarkable. Aside from ascribing this to be of divine providence, it is evidence of the centrality and importance of the concept of rest to the practice of Israel's faith.

The Land as a Type of Eden

In the midst of the second half of the book of Joshua, which details the apportioning of the land, Josh. 18 intrudes, telling the story of when the Israelites gathered together at Shiloh to set up the tent of meeting. Josh. 18:1 reads: "then the whole congregation of the sons of Israel assembled themselves at Shiloh, and set up the tent of meeting there; and the land was subdued before them." In a number of translations the point is sometimes missed, but there is a direct echo here of Gen. 1:28, nicely preserved by the NASB, in that the land lay "subdued" before them, just as Adam and Eve were commanded to subdue the land.[3] The connotations for the theme of rest though are not only limited to Genesis, for Shiloh is for the first time represented a type of temple or resting place in response to Deut. 12, where the Israelites would bring their sacrifices in worship.

Some see Josh. 18 as taking a central place within the chiastic structure organizing the section Josh. 13–21.

A 13:8–33 Transjordan for 2 ½ tribes

B 14:1–5 The principles of the division

C 14:6–15 Beginning: Caleb's inheritance

D 15:1–17:18 The lot for Judah and Joseph

E 18:1–10 The Tent of Meeting taken to Shiloh and the apportioning of the land

---

3. McConville and Williams, *Joshua*, 75.

> D' 18:11–19:48 The lot for the seven remaining tribes
>
> C' 19:49–51 Ending: Joshua's inheritance
>
> B' 20:1–6 God's fourth initiative: designating cities of refuge
>
> A' 20:7–21:42 Cities of refuge and Levitical cities

This chiasmus was first observed by Hendrik Koorevaar, who suggested that A and A' are grouped because neither the Transjordan tribes nor the Levites had a share in Canaan and that both B and B' are themed together by principles which govern the whole land of Israel.[4]

To identify Josh. 18:1–10 as the center piece of this section seems natural, as the institution of Shiloh as the center of Israelite worship functions as an obvious high point in the text.

Josh. 18:1 is no mere throw away comment; it touches upon the heart of Joshua's theological message. The land in the book of Joshua is symbolic of the garden of Eden which is established by the grace of God who alone gives it to the Israelites and by God's judgment upon the nations for the accumulation of their sin.

This verse wonderfully weaves together the themes of the central sanctuary, the land as inheritance, and the hope for Edenic restoration by the shared motif of rest. At the same time though it is doubtful whether the author of Joshua actually thought either that Shiloh was the fulfillment of Deut. 12 or that the conquest of Canaan finished the story which was begun in Genesis. For one thing the book remains clear that the land was not entirely taken and that the people still inevitably sinned. The book of Joshua then serves as an interpretive account of history, providing a paradigm for future generations to reflect on the ending to come.

Such an interpretation is in line also with the way that other parts of the Old Testament reflect on Israel's history. For instance, Ps 95:

> Today, if you would hear His voice,

4. Koorevaar, *De Opbouw van Het Boek Jozua*, 290.

Do not harden your hearts, as at Meribah,

As in the day of Massah in the wilderness,

When your fathers tested Me,

They tried Me, though they had seen My work.

For forty years I loathed that generation,

And said they are a people who err in their heart,

And they do not know My ways.

Therefore I swore in My anger,

Truly they shall not enter into My rest.

Psalm 95:7–11

In Psalm 95, the Israelites are reminded that entering God's rest is on the condition of obeying God's voice, where their ancestors' history puts forward a paradigm for their own journey towards entering God's spiritual rest.

Chaos and the Jordan Waters

When the Israelites came to cross the river Jordan into the land of Canaan, Joshua 3 records the event of God instructing Joshua and the Israelites saying:

> It shall come about when the soles of the feet of the priests who carry the ark of the Lord, the Lord of all the earth, rest in the waters of the Jordan, the waters of the Jordan will be cut off, and the waters which are flowing down from above will stand in one heap.

Joshua 3:13

It has been suggested that lying in the background to this story is the creation myth of Baal defeating Yam, whose name means Sea but is sometimes referred to as Nahar which means river.[5] This is possibly intimated in Psalm 74:

> Yet God is my king from of old,

5. McConville and Williams, *Joshua*, 19.

> Who works deeds of deliverance in the midst of the
> earth.
>
> You divided the sea by Your strength;
>
> You broke the heads of the sea monsters in the waters.
>
> You crushed the heads of Leviathan;
>
> You gave him as food for the creatures of the wilderness.
>
> You broke open springs and torrents;
>
> You dried up ever-flowing streams.
>
> Psalm 74:12–15

The psalmist creatively echoes mythic language to communicate the Lord's power over the cosmos. Yet it is questionable whether the writer of Joshua had likewise intended the account of this story as a polemic against Canaanite religion. All the same, Leviathan and the more common mention of the "waters" would seem to be the closest the Old Testament comes to playing upon the theme of "chaos."[6] To be clear though, it does so symbolically; the Old Testament nowhere presents the sea as a person with which God struggles and over which he eventually triumphs.[7] Rather only occasionally do the Old Testament writers borrow mythic language to make a counter claim that it is the Lord who supremely rules over all (e.g. Ps. 29; 93).

This theology of rest in the book of Joshua seems to be in continuity with that of the Pentateuch. There are no major new developments, but rather it traces the motif of rest through the events of the conquest with a continued focus on rest being the cessation of war, the inheritance of the land and the institution of the central sanctuary. At the same time there is the continued recognition closely associating the receipt of God's rest with promise of God's word.

---

6. Day, *God's Conflict with the Dragon and the Sea*, 22.

7. Watson, *Chaos Uncreated*, 4.

Chapter 8

In the Days when the Judges Ruled

This chapter will look at "rest" in the monarchic period, namely the books of Judges and Ruth which are commonly dated to this period and the book of Samuel. The book of Samuel and specifically 2 Sam. 7, is also included in this chapter, given the "to this day" reference in 1 Sam. 27:6,[1] which makes an early monarchic date very likely.[2]

Rest in the Book of Judges

It is generally understood that the book of Judges preserves the stories of various deliverers and frames these stories using "Deuteronomic language" during the introductory and concluding statements, such as "the Lord raised up a deliverer," "the sons of Israel cried out the Lord," "the Lord gave them into the hands of," and of particular interest here the formula "the land had rest for (x) years."[3] As the book progresses there is a breakdown in the use these formulas which parallels Israel's spiritual disintegration.[4] The rest formula also follows this pattern; it is used to conclude

---

1. 1 Sam. 27:6 states that the town of Ziklag was ruled by the kings of Judah "to this day," yet Ziklag was taken by the Pharaoh Shishak of Egypt ca. 925 BC.

2. Tsumura, *Book of 1 Samuel*, 612.

3. Webb, *Book of Judges*, 43.

4. Exum, "The Centre Cannot Hold."

the sections of the earlier judges through to Gideon, but is then dropped for the remainder of the book.

The use of the formula at the end of the Gideon narrative is quite surprising, even ironic. Gideon had requested the Israelites' golden earrings with which he made an ephod:

> Gideon made it into an ephod, and placed it in his city, Ophrah, and all Israel played the harlot with it there, so that it became a snare to Gideon and his household.
>
> So Midian was subdued before the sons of Israel, and they did not lift up their heads anymore. And the land was undisturbed for forty years in the days of Gideon.
>
> Judges 8:27–28

Whether or not Gideon intended the ephod to become an idol, he is implicated in the people's sin. The following note then about Midian being subdued and the land having rest is almost ironic; for the absence of the rest formula in the following sections is indicative of the extent of Israel's sinfulness. There is an implicit connection here between rest and being obedient to the word of the Lord. The nations were left in the land in order to test Israel, to see if they will walk in the ways of the Lord (Jdg. 2:20–23). When the people return to the Lord, the land had rest from their enemies, but when they turned away from the Lord's commands, the descent into idolatry left the land without rest.

It is striking that all throughout the book of Judges it is the land which is said to have rest. Certainly the land here is being personified as being the political territory of Israel, because the rest (*sqt*) is the cessation of war.[5] Nevertheless, at other points it is clear that land requires a Sabbath rest and the point that God's rest is for the whole of creation, may be implicit within the metaphor.

Near the end of the book, the story of the Danites' conquest and occupation of Laish is recorded. The tribe of Dan, having failed to acquire their allotted inheritance in the west, migrates towards Laish in the west and spy out the land.[6] The Sidonians living

---

5. Sasson, *Judges 1–12*, 216.

6. Note that the name of Manoah, meaning resting place, the father of

in Laish though were quiet (*sqt*) and peaceful. These people are not implicated in the same mire of sin which brought God's judgment on the seven nations living in the land of Canaan. It is possible that there is an intentional play on words here; the Sidonians were experiencing the rest which the Lord intended for the tribe of Dan, yet the Danites' failure to obey God's word deprives not only themselves but also the Sidonians from experiencing rest.[7]

Rest and the Covenant with David

The period of the judges was a time of disturbance — a view taken both by the book of Judges and here in 2 Sam. 7 where God responds to David's proposal to build a temple through the prophet Nathan:

> Now it came about when the king lived in his house, and the Lord had given him rest on every side from all his enemies, that the king said to Nathan the prophet, "See now, I dwell in a house of cedar, but the ark of God dwells within tent curtains." Nathan said to the king, "Go, do all that is in your mind, for the Lord is with you."
>
> But in the same night the word of the Lord came to Nathan, saying, "Go and say to My servant David, 'Thus says the Lord, "Are you the one who should build Me a house to dwell in?
>
> "Now therefore, thus you shall say to My servant David, 'Thus says the Lord of hosts, "I took you from the pasture, from following the sheep, to be ruler over My people Israel. I have been with you wherever you have gone and have cut off all your enemies from before you; and I will make you a great name, like the names of the great men who are on the earth. I will also appoint a place for My people Israel and will plant them, that they may live in their own place and not be disturbed again, nor will the wicked afflict them any more as formerly,

---

Samson from the tribe of Dan may be ironical because Dan never received her inheritance. Webb, *Book of Judges*, 350.

7. Butler, *Judges*, 394.

even from the day that I commanded judges to be over
My people Israel; and I will give you rest from all your
enemies. The Lord also declares to you that the Lord will
make a house for you. When your days are complete and
you lie down with your fathers, I will raise up your descendant after you, who will come forth from you, and
I will establish his kingdom. He shall build a house for
My name, and I will establish the throne of his kingdom
forever. I will be a father to him and he will be a son to
Me; when he commits iniquity, I will correct him with
the rod of men and the strokes of the sons of men, but
My lovingkindness shall not depart from him, as I took it
away from Saul, whom I removed from before you. Your
house and your kingdom shall endure before Me forever;
your throne shall be established forever."'"

2 Samuel 7:1–5, 8–16

The time of the judges is specifically contrasted with the promised
to David and his offspring, it was a time of disturbance and af-
fliction, but God promises rest, being free from the attack of an
enemy. This promise will be brought about through a leader, David's son, who will build the temple and sit enthroned over this
kingdom forever. Yet this son will be sinful by nature and in need
of the Lord's correction, so there is already a hint that the birth of
David's son is not the ultimate rest, but in some way prefigures it,
even as Joshua did, for sin is not consonant with God's eternal rest.

It would not of course be surprising that the subject of rest
should arise with David's deciding to build a temple for the Lord.
It was common in the ancient Near East for temples, the resting
places and thrones of gods, to be constructed by a king in order
to secure favor. Rather, what would have been surprising at least
for the ancient Mesopotamians is the Lord's response to David; for
all the magnificent promises that the Lord gives to David, none
of them is conditioned by David doing anything in return but are
given freely. In fact it is not David who will build God's house but
God has chosen to build David's house. Similarly it is not man who
establishes God's rest but God who establishes his rest and grants it
freely, even as he has done from the beginning.

Rest is the fruit of God being faithful to his own word, not the achievement of man. This truth is again clearly seen in this passage. Even in the first verse, God gave David rest on every side, echoing Deut. 12:10, something which precedes his choosing of a place for his name to dwell. The promise of rest given to David is relentless and undeserved grace where the assurance of God's goodness is God himself not David; this point is in no way lost on David who recognizes this in his prayer which follows (2 Sam. 7:18ff). It is a promise which will continue even in the face of his descendants' sin and rebellion.

God's promise and gift of rest is not exclusive only to David and his descendants. The king is the representative of the nation, so even as God gives David rest from all his enemies, this rest is experienced by all the nation of Israel.[8] More than this though, it is a rest offered to all who turn to him.

Rest in the Book of Ruth

The book of Ruth takes place "in the days when the judges ruled," in the midst of Israel's spiritual depravity but also at a time of famine and hardship. The narrative follows the story of Naomi, an Israelite woman living in Moab who had lost her husband and her two sons, as well as the security and provision they brought. In turning to go back to Israel and expecting to part company with to her Moabite daughters-in-law she says to them: "may the Lord grant that you may find rest, each in the house of her husband" (Ruth 1:9).

The "rest" (*nuah*) here is freely given by the Lord and it is not thought of as being limited only for Israelites. These Moabite women, Orpah and Ruth — even these women from the country of Moab, which was under God's judgment (Deut. 23:3) — can be recipients of God's rest. The prayer is clearly that *the Lord* would grant them rest, not that they would experience rest in returning to Moab and their idols. This affirms the missional function of Israel's

8. Evans, *1 and 2 Samuel*, 168.

theology of rest, which was to be freely offered to all peoples yet demanded a radical commitment to Israel's monolatry; as was detailed earlier, Israel's worldview so uniquely diverged from others that it was not possible to merely assimilate it within an existing mythic one.

Of course Ruth goes with Naomi and the story follows the events which provide an answer to Naomi's prayer for Ruth. Ruth's marriage to Boaz is explicitly associated with this rest (*nuah*), here translated "security:" "then Naomi her mother-in-law said to her, 'My daughter, shall I not seek security for you, that it may be well with you?'" (Ruth 3:1).

Remarkably in the midst of the judges, when the land is no longer experiencing the Lord's rest, rest was granted to this helpless Moabite woman and through her seed to the whole of Israel.

God's rest is the fruit of God's word, it embodies a message for the nations and it projects a vision of an eternal rest. This is all entirely consistent with the theology of rest observed in the Torah and the book of Joshua. It is again remarkable that Israel's theology of rest should hold through the changes of Israel's history and is testament to the importance and centrality of the concept of "rest" in Israel's faith.

The unique addition arising from this period in Israel's history is the linking of God's rest with a future descendant of David. This is also taken up in Isaiah, "then in that day, the nations will resort to the root of Jesse, who will stand as a signal for the peoples; and His resting place will be glorious" (Isaiah. 11:10).[9] The vision of re-creation and rest, projected by Israel's theology of land and of sanctuary are woven together and continued explicitly in the future descendant of King David, a view which was maintained even during the exile and the seeming end of David's line; for from the root of Jesse, the messiah would come forth.

---

9. Note a possible play on words. In Is. 11:2 it is him on whom the spirit "rests."

Chapter 9

Rest and the Temple

The temple's layout and size closely resembles the temples of Tell Tayinat in the south east of modern day Turkey and Ain Dara which is nearby in Syria.[1] On the surface level, Solomon's temple not only in layout but also in its construction, was not particularly unique; it was normal for kings and leaders to commission the building of temples and this happened all across the ancient Near East right down until the time of the Greeks and Romans.

Common to most of these designs is that they claim to be the place of the primordial hill, upon which the particular deity dwelt. This is the hill which emerged from the seas of chaos, and represents the rest created out of its midst. It is a principle almost universally seen in the Egyptian temples, for example at Karnak where the walls border off the waters and also in Babylon with the Esagila temple.[2]

At least superficially Solomon's temple bears a resemblance to the temples of the nations, but this does not necessitate understanding Solomon's temple to be a copy and imitation of the nations', for there are certainly unique features to Israel's temple design and theology. A balance needs to be maintained; Israel shared what has been called a "common cognitive environment" with her neighbors,[3] which here extends to the structure and

1. Monson, "The Temple of Solomon: Heart of Jerusalem."
2. Keel, *The Symbolism of the Biblical World*, 113.
3. Walton, *Ancient Near Eastern Thought*, 332.

layout of her temple, and yet at the same time within this shared cultural heritage Israel held onto a radically different worldview. Perhaps here it is helpful to reiterate John Oswalt's judgment; Israel's message was not unique because it was completely unrelated to the world in which she lived, but rather it was unique because at the same time as using concepts and forms familiar to the world it communicated a message diametrically opposed to the worldview of the nations.[4]

With regards to the construction of the temple, of course there are differences in the details of the layout and design of the temple, for example the Edenic symbolism which was noted also in the tabernacle's design. Yet even more than this, there are huge differences underlying the purpose and existence of Solomon's temple; the temple was not understood to secure God's favor but rather was symbolic of his grace and pointed forward to the eternal rest to come and which was freely offered to all.

The particularities of Israel's faith and her theological basis for building the temple were widely known, not just within Israel but also among the nations. Solomon's interaction with the King of Tyre evidences this to be true:

> Then Solomon sent word to Hiram, saying, "You know that David my father was unable to build a house for the name of the Lord his God because of the wars which surrounded him, until the Lord put them under the soles of his feet. But now the Lord my God has given me rest on every side; there is neither adversary nor misfortune. Behold, I intend to build a house for the name of the Lord my God, as the Lord spoke to David my father, saying, 'Your son, whom I will set on your throne in your place, he will build the house for My name.'"

1 Kings 5:2–5

Solomon assumes that Hiram is aware of God's covenant with David and the interaction which follows in the text would not make sense if the assumption was not true. The account of the temple

---

4. Oswalt, *Bible among the Myths*, 103.

construction, beginning with Solomon making provision for it through the trade agreements with Tyre, is intensely theological. This is true even of detailed record of the temple design; it is not merely an architectural blueprint, because there is not enough detail.[5] The text shows God fulfilling his word, both to Moses in constructing a resting place in the likeness of the tabernacle upon which God places his name, and to Solomon in granting him wisdom beyond that of anyone else. More than this though the temple stands as a testament to God's word; pointing forward to the re-creation and eternal rest to come, an idea which is explored later in the chapter.

Solomon's Prayer of Dedication

At the dedication of the temple, Solomon addresses God and requests that God hears the prayers asking for forgiveness, then Solomon gives seven different cases in which a person might pray towards the temple in repentance (1 Kgs. 8:31–53):

1. When a man sins against his neighbor (vv. 31–32).
2. When Israel are defeated by an enemy because they have sinned (vv. 33–34).
3. When there is no rain because Israel has sinned (vv. 35–36).
4. When there is famine because of Israel's sin (vv. 37–40).
5. When a foreigner comes from a foreign land (vv. 41–43).
6. When Israel goes out to battle (vv. 44–45).
7. Whenever anyone sins against you and cries out in repentance (vv. 46–53).

Following this prayer, Solomon cries out in praise to God for granting his people rest:

> When Solomon had finished praying this entire prayer and supplication to the Lord, he arose from before the

5. Beal, *1 and 2 Kings*, 118.

altar of the Lord, from kneeling on his knees with his hands spread toward heaven. And he stood and blessed all the assembly of Israel with a loud voice, saying:

"Blessed be the Lord, who has given rest to His people Israel, according to all that He promised; not one word has failed of all His good promise, which He promised through Moses His servant. May the Lord our God be with us, as He was with our fathers; may He not leave us or forsake us, that He may incline our hearts to Himself, to walk in all His ways and to keep His commandments and His statutes and His ordinances, which He commanded our fathers. And may these words of mine, with which I have made supplication before the Lord, be near to the Lord our God day and night, that He may maintain the cause of His servant and the cause of His people Israel, as each day requires, so that all the peoples of the earth may know that the Lord is God; there is no one else. Let your heart therefore be wholly devoted to the Lord our God, to walk in His statutes and to keep His commandments, as at this day."

1 Kings 8:54–61

This text elucidates a number of key points for this study. Firstly, it underlines the relationship between rest and the forgiveness of sin. Sin is the reason why creation does not experience God's rest as he intended and ultimately his rest will not be fully established until sin is completely done away with and all things are made new. Tightly connected to this point, is the fact that rest is brought about by God's word. People can experience God's rest when they are obedient to his word, such obedience is the antithesis of sin. Yet at the same time, his rest is not governed by the acts of men but because God himself has spoken and promised. God is the agent bringing forth his rest; if a person walks according to God's word it is because God has inclined that man's heart to do so. Consequently, God's rest is not earned it is freely given to any who repent. Regardless of the conditions a person finds himself in as a result of his sin and regardless of ethnicity, God's grace and free offer of rest is openly given to all who would repent.

It has been suggested by some source critical scholars that the original Deuteronomist held a view where the era of rest was meant to commence after the conquest of Israel and then the revised vision held that this rest was ushered in during Solomon's days.[6] Now it has already been argued earlier in this study that the Israelites never actually thought that the rest was established by the conquest; but there is a question here whether or not the author or final editor of Kings thought of the era of rest being ushered in by Solomon's temple? Absolutely not. To begin with the remainder of the narrative in Kings follows Israel's story into exile. More than this though the account of the temple construction retains a critical voice; the temple is achieved through forced labor which later fuels a rebellion (1 Kgs. 12), then there is Solomon's sour dealings with Hiram King of Tyre (1 Kgs. 9:11–14), the royal palace is comparatively grander than the temple (1 Kgs. 9:10) and there is potential for the temple to be rejected by the Lord (1Kgs. 9:8), so this hardly seems the place of the Lord's everlasting rest and rule.

Israelites at the time of the exile believed that the temple was the guarantee of Judah's ongoing protection from the Lord, but the book of Kings itself makes clear that it is only obedience to God's word which acts as a guarantor:

> Now the word of the Lord came to Solomon saying, "Concerning this house which you are building, if you will walk in My statutes and execute My ordinances and keep all My commandments by walking in them, then I will carry out My word with you which I spoke to David your father. I will dwell among the sons of Israel, and will not forsake My people Israel."

1 Kings 6:11–13

All of this makes clear that the Israelites did not understand Solomon to be initiating a new era of rest, rather only that the temple prefigured the coming rule and rest of God which they expected to be fully established at the end.

---

6. Cogan, *1 Kings*, 288.

Temple Rest and the Eschaton

The temple construction started in the 480th year after the Exodus (1 Kgs. 6:1), which has the symbolic value of being twelve lots of forty, and took just over seven years to complete, in the eighth month of Solomon's eleventh year (1 Kgs. 6:38). Yet the temple was dedicated in the seventh month (1 Kgs. 8:2), meaning that the Israelites waited a full eleven months before consecrating it. The reason for waiting was to align the dedication of the temple with the Feast of Tabernacles, which as suggested earlier in the study carries eschatological overtones. Though others such as Rubenstein have argued that Solomon chose the Feast of Tabernacles because it was the leading pilgrimage ceremony, he presupposes that Israel developed its eschatology later in her history,[7] a view that this study has sought to argue against. In truth, it is not known how well attended the various festivals were at different points in Israel's history, nor is this a reason given in the text, but the references to the nations; the Canaanite month of Elthanim (1 Kgs. 6:1), and the foreigner which the Lord answers (1 Kgs. 8:41–43) signal the festival's eschatological concern in this passage.[8] Within this record the importance of the number seven is notable, as well as Solomon's seven requests, there are seven days of dedication, followed by seven days for the Feast of Tabernacles which is the seventh feast in the seventh month.

The Zion theology emanating from the temple construction, existing before the second temple period, also had a clear eschatological focus. For instance the book of Micah records this oracle:

---

7. Rubenstein, "Sukkot, Eschatology and Zechariah 14," 188.

8. Beal, *1 and 2 Kings*, 135.

And it will come about in the last days
That the mountain of the house of the Lord
Will be established as the chief of the mountains.
It will be raised above the hills,
And the peoples will stream to it.
Many nations will come and say,
"Come and let us go up to the mountain of the Lord
And to the house of the God of Jacob,
That He may teach us about His ways
And that we may walk in His paths."
For from Zion will go forth the law,
Even the word of the Lord from Jerusalem.
And He will judge between many peoples
And render decisions for mighty, distant nations.
Then they will hammer their swords into plowshares
And their spears into pruning hooks;
Nation will not lift up sword against nation,
And never again will they train for war.
Each of them will sit under his vine
And under his fig tree,
With no one to make them afraid,
For the mouth of the Lord of hosts has spoken.
Though all the peoples walk
Each in the name of his god,
As for us, we will walk
In the name of the Lord our God forever and ever.
"In that day," declares the Lord,
"I will assemble the lame
And gather the outcasts,
Even those whom I have afflicted.
"I will make the lame a remnant

And the outcasts a strong nation,

And the Lord will reign over them in Mount Zion

From now on and forever.

"As for you, tower of the flock,

Hill of the daughter of Zion,

To you it will come—

Even the former dominion will come,

The kingdom of the daughter of Jerusalem."

Micah 4:1–8

Coming immediately after Micah's prophecy declaring the coming destruction of Jerusalem where the temple will become a heap of ruins, this oracle pictures Zion rising above all other hills. Of course Zion is not actually the highest mountain in the region, but the point is that in an apocalyptic moment it would be raised higher than any other.[9] At the end of time the truth that the Lord reigns over all will become manifest and all peoples will gather to worship him. For Micah, Solomon's temple served to prefigure and point to the Lord's eternal throne and coming kingdom which will be established at the end.

The Temple of Solomon embodied a message for the nations: God will establish his resting place at a future unspecified time, his rest will be glorious and it is freely offered to all people. The long expected building of the temple at a place chosen by God, was built by Solomon in accordance to God's word. Yet the author and reader remain under no illusion, it is a mere sign of the coming rest, eternal and free from sin.

9. Cross, *Canaanite Myth and Hebrew Epic*, 142.

Chapter 10

Rest and Judgment

A ssociating God's rest with his judgment at this point should not be particularly surprising. It has already been observed in the story of Noah, in the conquest of the land of Canaan and in the time of the judges. This chapter looks at the theme of rest in the oracles of judgment spoken by the prophets and then proceeds to look at rest within the prophetic vision of eschatological judgment and re-creation.

God's Judgment as Life without Rest

Israel was assured that upon straying from God's word, they would receive his judgment. It should be of no surprise then that this rebellion entails restlessness because rest is the product of obedience to God's word. God's word to Ahaz and the rulers of the day was that if they in repentance trusted in God rather than the nations, then they would find rest (Is. 30:15). However God's word which could potentially have been a source of rest, became words of judgment:

> Indeed, He will speak to this people
>
> Through stammering lips and a foreign tongue,
>
> He who said to them, "Here is rest, give rest to the weary,"
>
> And, "Here is repose," but they would not listen.

> So the word of the Lord to them will be,
>
> "Order on order, order on order,
>
> Line on line, line on line,
>
> A little here, a little there,"
>
> That they may go and stumble backward, be broken,
> snared and taken captive."
>
> Isaiah 28:11–13

Yet Israel chose to trust in the nations rather than the Lord and as such Isaiah informs them that they will hear God's judgment from the lips of foreigners. Similarly, God spoke through the prophet Jeremiah:

> Thus says the Lord,
>
> "Stand by the ways and see and ask for the ancient paths,
>
> Where the good way is, and walk in it;
>
> And you will find rest for your souls.
>
> But they said, 'We will not walk in it.'
>
> "And I set watchmen over you, saying,
>
> 'Listen to the sound of the trumpet!'
>
> But they said, 'We will not listen.'"
>
> Jeremiah 6:16–17

Following these verses, God outlines the consequent judgment for rebelling against God's word. God spoke both through the Torah, the ancient path and prophets such as Isaiah, watchmen, but Israel would not listen; the promise was rest but in its stead Israel faced judgment. There are numerous places which contrast God's rest and God's judgment, or make clear that God's judgment is the absence of rest (e.g. Mic. 2:10, Lam. 1:3; 5:5, Hab. 2:5, et.al). Yet these two references have been cited because in addition to showing that rest is the antithesis of God's judgment, they so clearly substantiate the point that rest is the product of obeying God's word. The place of rest in the language of judgment is not only reserved for

Israel though. For instance Isaiah makes known God's intention to deprive the nations of rest in his oracle against Tyre and Sidon:

> He has stretched His hand out over the sea,
>
> He has made the kingdoms tremble;
>
> The Lord has given a command concerning Canaan to demolish its strongholds.
>
> He has said, "You shall exult no more, O crushed virgin daughter of Sidon.
>
> Arise, pass over to Cyprus; even there you will find no rest."
>
> Isaiah 23:11–12

Of course the prophets did not only bring a message of judgment, they also brought a message of hope and future restoration, reassuring people that God had not completely abandoned his creation:

> When the Lord will have compassion on Jacob and again choose Israel, and settle them in their own land, then strangers will join them and attach themselves to the house of Jacob. The peoples will take them along and bring them to their place, and the house of Israel will possess them as an inheritance in the land of the Lord as male servants and female servants; and they will take their captors captive and will rule over their oppressors.
>
> And it will be in the day when the Lord gives you rest from your pain and turmoil and harsh service in which you have been enslaved.
>
> Isaiah 14:1–3

Isaiah 14 outlines the future judgment of Babylon and the rejoicing when the house of Jacob is freed from the slavery that she will experience under Babylon. God will once again give them rest in the land and the amazing promise is that they will be joined by members of other nations. God's word is the promise of rest and it is a promise for all peoples. In all of this it must of course be remembered that Old Testament prophecy has on its horizon the eschaton. So when the prophets pronounce judgment it is but a precursor to the coming day of the Lord. Similarly, when the hope of rest is held out, it should point the reader to the greater promise of eternal rest. This claim can be observed in scripture itself, upon looking at the connection between rest and the resurrection.

Rest and the Resurrection

The most explicit verse connecting "rest" to the resurrection, is found at the very end of the book of Daniel, Dan. 12:13: "but as for you, go your way to the end; then you will enter into rest and rise again for your allotted portion at the end of the age." Coming after the command for Daniel to "seal up the words of this book," in the midst of Daniel's confusion and awareness of coming hardships, these words provide a comfort and assurance of God's rest.

These verses in Daniel make clear that there will be an end and that God's word will stand forever. Rest is here spoken of in terms of a sleep which will last until the end. Sleep is an appropriate metaphor because it contains the idea of rising again,[1] and it entails not being arrested by the burden of sin in death. This is seen to be true in turning to Isaiah 57, with the promise of healing for the righteous (Is. 57:18) and the rest to come:

> For the righteous man is taken away from evil,
>
> He enters into peace;
>
> They rest in their beds,
>
> Each one who walked in his upright way.
>
> Isaiah 57:1b-2

"Beds" might otherwise be translated "graves" as it is in other translations. The purpose in translating it "beds" though is not to limit this rest to an earthly sense, but rather to make it clear that this rest involves more than just death, indeed the mention of peace implies something of a reward.[2] This sense is also endorsed

1. Baldwin, *Daniel*, 204.
2. Oswalt, *The Book of Isaiah*, 471.

by an appreciation of the wider context; in that Is. 57:1–2 together with its parallel in Is. 57:20–21 frame the oracle:[3]

A Peace and rest for the righteous (1–2)

　B The prostitute and her family (3–13d)

　　B^1 The family (3–5)

　　　B^2 The prostitute's ways (6–13d)

　　　　C Conclusion and Transition: trust and inheritance (13ef)

　　　　C' Transition and Introduction: the homeward road (14)

　　　B' The Lord and his household (15–19)

　　　$B^{1'}$ The holy one and his household (15)

　　　$B^{2'}$ The Lord's work: healing, comforting, peace (16–19)

A' The impossibility of peace and rest for the wicked (20–21)

Rest is something the righteous enjoy from death and even onwards beyond the end of the age, whereas the wicked have no peace or rest but rather experience God's judgment:

But the wicked are like the tossing sea,

For it cannot be quiet,

And its waters toss up refuse and mud.

"There is no peace," says my God, "for the wicked."

Isaiah 57:20–21

This understanding of rest in entirely consistent with what has been observed up to this point: judgment on sin is the antithesis of the rest resulting from obedience to God's word. The original sin in Eden interrupted God's rest, yet the Israelites believed that God forgave sin and offered the promise of eternal rest for all who

3. Motyer, *The Prophecy of Isaiah*, 470.

would trust in his word and looked forward to a time when the end would be like the beginning, being restored to its original state.[4]

The purpose of the eschaton within the prophetic message, was not so much to endorse escapism or create some abstract utopia, but rather to cause people to turn to God in that moment and consider the ethical implications for living in a present sin-stained world.[5] As such the prophets reiterate that this message of rest is freely offered to all nations, yet rejection and continued rebellion against the creator left them facing certain judgment. Indeed this is not merely a possibility but an inevitability; one day the Lord will gather at his resting place in Zion people from all nations. He will create the new heavens and the new earth, where there will be great rejoicing and where the toil and anguish will be remembered no more (Is. 65).

4. Levenson, "The Temple and the World."

5. Wright, *Old Testament Ethics for the People of God*, 186.

Chapter 11

Purim and the Rest of God

The events surrounding the inauguration of the festival of the Purim are recorded in the story of Esther. As was the case with the holy days set forth in the Torah, so it is the case with the festival of the Purim; the theme of rest holds a very significant place in understanding the meaning of the festival. The interplay already observed between God's rest, his word, his judgment, and the eschatological hope are all evidenced further in the book of Esther. Despite the fact that God does not speak in course of the narrative, it is still his word which drives the story.

The command given to blot out the Amalekites has already been noted earlier in the study: "when the Lord your God gives you rest from all the enemies around you in the land he is giving you to possess as an inheritance, you shall blot out the name of Amalek from under heaven. Do not forget!" (Deut. 25:19). Despite God's command though the Israelites did forget and this is epitomized by the events many years later when Saul fights the Amalekites:

> Then Saul attacked the Amalekites all the way from Havilah to Shur, near the eastern border of Egypt. He took Agag king of the Amalekites alive, and all his people he totally destroyed with the sword. But Saul and the army spared Agag and the best of the sheep and cattle, the fat calves and lambs – everything that was good. These they were unwilling to destroy completely, but everything that was despised and weak they totally destroyed.

> Then the word of the Lord came to Samuel: "I regret that I have made Saul king, because he has turned away from me and has not carried out my instructions." Samuel was angry, and he cried out to the Lord all that night.

1 Samuel 15:7–11

This is the context for the story of Esther. While in exile in Persia, a descendant of Agag, Haman the Agagite, seizes an opportunity to persecute the Jews and attempts to wipe them out. The story then tells of remarkable events which turn the tables; Haman is hanged and Mordecai receives authority, those who planned to annihilate the Jews are themselves annihilated. This is actualized by the request of Queen Esther and the granting of that request by King Xerxes.

The writer does not intend to paint Esther here as merciless and unforgiving but rather she is seen as being faithful to God's word. There is no question about this, the annihilation against their enemies is seen positively and the day is to be celebrated annually forevermore.

Although Mordecai's official decree permits the taking of plunder, reflecting a reversal of Haman's decree against the Jews, the writer is keen to point out that no plunder was taken (Est, 9:10, 15, 16). The text therefore seeks to demonstrate that those carrying out Mordecai's decree were aware that this was an act of holy war and in line with God's word, not just an aggressive and emotional reaction.

> Meanwhile, the remainder of the Jews who were in the king's provinces also assembled to protect themselves and get relief from their enemies. They killed seventy-five thousand of them but did not lay their hands on the plunder. This happened on the thirteenth day of the month of Adar, and on the fourteenth they rested and made it a day of feasting and joy.
>
> The Jews in Susa, however, had assembled on the thirteenth and fourteenth, and then on the fifteenth they rested and made it a day of feasting and joy.

> That is why rural Jews—those living in villages—observe the fourteenth of the month of Adar as a day of joy and feasting, a day for giving presents to each other.
>
> Mordecai recorded these events, and he sent letters to all the Jews throughout the provinces of King Xerxes, near and far, that they should celebrate annually the fourteenth and fifteenth days of the month of Adar as the time when the Jews got relief from their enemies, and as the month when their sorrow was turned into joy and their mourning into a day of celebration. He wrote to them to observe the days as days of feasting and joy and giving presents of food to one another and gifts to the poor.

Esther 9:16–22

Notice the importance of the theme of rest, here translated "relief" by the NASB in Est. 9:22. The Jews protected themselves and gained rest from their enemies (Est. 9:16, 22), the outworking of God's word against Amalek. As a result this day was forever to be celebrated as a day of rest; a day of feasting and celebration of gift giving and joy.

Perhaps it can be venturesomely suggested that the festival points forward to the future eschatological joy and feasting, when judgment will come upon all God's enemies and his people are given rest. Just as it was with the Feast of Tabernacles with its mandatory joy and celebration, so Purim likewise points the participant towards the future end time hope and accompanying joy. Purim was to be a time of meditating upon God's faithfulness to his word in bringing about his promised rest, and of looking forward in expectation to the coming rest.

It is true that the text never explicitly warrants an eschatological interpretation, that such an argument is impossible to make from Esther alone and that such an interpretation is not commonplace.[1] Essentially the argument relies on the premises

---

1. Note the exception of a recent article: Duguid, "But Did They Live Happily Ever After? Eschatology in the Book of Esther." Duguid similarly points to "rest" in the concluding section of the book to suggest that there are eschatological overtones to Esther's message.

that Israel's theology of rest had eschatological overtones and that the festival's joy, which similarly marks the feast of tabernacles, is an indication of its end-time focus. These are premises which cannot be argued solely from the book of Esther and admittedly require a positive evaluation of the arguments put forward in the study up until this point. Yet at the same time, it should be noted that the observations taken regarding rest in the book of Esther adds weight to the central hypothesis, that there is one theology of rest; by affirming the relationship between God's word and his rest and that the tentative eschatological interpretation of Esther is consistent within the hypothesis itself .

The story of Esther stresses the sovereignty of God, for while he does not speak, nor is he mentioned, his word governs the events and leads them toward their inevitable conclusion, God's rest. Inevitable is the right word here, because it reflects the book's portrayal of God's sovereignty:

> Then Mordecai told them to reply to Esther, "Do not imagine that you in the king's palace can escape any more than all the Jews. For if you remain silent at this time, relief and deliverance will arise for the Jews from another place and you and your father's house will perish. And who knows whether you have not attained royalty for such a time as this?"

Esther 4:13–14

Mordecai is here encouraging Esther to daringly approach the king and ask for his favor; the question is not whether the Jews will experience God's deliverance but whether Esther herself wishes to enjoy it. It should be noted that the text almost goes out of its way not to mention God here, by refusing to detail where and how this relief and deliverance would come.[2] Yet this touches upon one of the key theological themes in the book — the question as to whether God is present — and so commentators widely recognize that God is intentionally not mentioned here by the author.[3] For

---

2. Reid, *Esther*, 104.
3. Jobes, *Esther*, 44.

what reason though does Mordecai have such confidence that deliverance will indeed come? Perhaps it would be objected that this is to paint Mordecai as a man of faith beyond what the text actually discloses, but it is fitting the wider context of scripture to understand that his confidence comes from a belief in God's faithfulness both to his word and his people.[4]

The book of Esther holds to an understanding of rest shared by the rest of the canon. It is a rest which will be enjoyed ultimately after a time of judgment, just as was seen with the story of Noah and Israel's conquest of the land and it is a rest which is guaranteed by the certainty of God's word.

4. Bush, *Ruth-Esther*, 396.

Chapter 12

Rest in the Book of Chronicles

The book of Chronicles was of course written after the exile and retells Israel's history, tracing the story through the Kingdom of Judah. It holds to a messianic expectation in line with the prophets, where the coming messiah would be a descendant of David and looks forward in expectation to the rest that he would bring.

God's Covenant with David

> And it came about, when David dwelt in his house, that David said to Nathan the prophet, "Behold, I am dwelling in a house of cedar, but the ark of the covenant of the Lord is under curtains." Then Nathan said to David, "Do all that is in your heart, for God is with you."
>
> It came about the same night that the word of God came to Nathan, saying, "Go and tell David My servant, 'Thus says the Lord, "You shall not build a house for Me to dwell in; for I have not dwelt in a house since the day that I brought up Israel to this day, but I have gone from tent to tent and from one dwelling place to another. In all places where I have walked with all Israel, have I spoken a word with any of the judges of Israel, whom I commanded to shepherd My people, saying, 'Why have you not built for Me a house of cedar?'"' Now, therefore, thus shall you say to My servant David, 'Thus says the Lord of hosts, "I took you from the pasture, from following the sheep, to be leader over My people Israel. I have been with you

wherever you have gone, and have cut off all your enemies from before you; and I will make you a name like the name of the great ones who are in the earth. I will appoint a place for My people Israel, and will plant them, so that they may dwell in their own place and not be moved again; and the wicked will not waste them anymore as formerly, even from the day that I commanded judges to be over My people Israel. And I will subdue all your enemies.

Moreover, I tell you that the Lord will build a house for you. When your days are fulfilled that you must go to be with your fathers, that I will set up one of your descendants after you, who will be of your sons; and I will establish his kingdom. He shall build for Me a house, and I will establish his throne forever. I will be his father and he shall be My son; and I will not take My loving-kindness away from him, as I took it from him who was before you. But I will settle him in My house and in My kingdom forever, and his throne shall be established for-ever."'" According to all these words and according to all this vision, so Nathan spoke to David.

1 Chronicles 17:1–15

1 Chr. 17:1–15 is almost verbatim the same as 2 Sam. 7:1–17, but for some very small yet significant changes; the Chronicler re-moves any mention of "rest," David's descendant becomes one of his descendants and the clause "when he commits iniquity, I will correct him with the rod of men" (2 Sam. 7:14) is omitted.

The chronicler abstains from mentioning "rest." In the open-ing verse which is otherwise the same as 2 Sam. 7 but for the omission of "and the Lord had given him rest on every side" and similarly David is not promised rest from his enemies (2 Sam. 7:11) but rather that they will be subdued (1 Chr. 17:11). This is certainly not because "rest" was not an important concept to the Chronicler, rest is in fact a central motif, as shall be seen. The reason that "rest" is omitted from 1 Chr. 17 is because David is presented as a man of war (1 Chr. 22:8; 28:3), not of rest.[1] The point that the Chronicler makes though is not so much that the temple construction had to

1. Braun, 1 Chronicles, 198.

be delayed because David had been involved in war.[2] Rather the emphasis is on David's unworthiness to build the temple, he is unfit because he is a "man of war." The Chronicler does not conceive of a messianic rest brought about through violence.

In contrast to David, the man of war, Solomon ,the descendant of David, is a "man of rest" (1 Chr. 22:9). This contrast is intentionally set up by the Chronicler, depicting Solomon as a type, someone who is worthy to establish God's resting place.[3] Solomon is presented by the chronicler as the perfect and sinless son of David, whose faults are not mentioned in Chronicles. This is not a case of the Chronicler attempting to rewrite history, rather he expects the reader to already know the details of Israel's history and of God's covenantal promise to David and to recognize cases of divergence. Solomon in the book of Chronicles, points forward to a sinless and peaceful descendant of David, who will establish the rest promised to David.

Rest in the Book of Chronicles

Rest is a prominent theme in the book of Chronicles; the temple construction is not surprisingly littered with references to rest (e.g. 1 Chr. 22:9; 23:25; 28:2 et al.)[4] and the land experiences rest under the reigns of Abijah (2 Chr. 14:6), Asa (2 Chr. 15:15) and Jehoshaphat (2 Chr. 20:30).

Amongst these texts though, there are a couple which deserve special mention because they clearly affirm the link between God's rest and God's word. The first of these is to be found in Solomon's dedication of the temple:

> "Now, O my God, I pray, let Your eyes be open and Your ears attentive to the prayer offered in this place.
> "Now therefore arise, O Lord God, to Your resting place, You and the ark of Your might; let Your priests, O

2. Ibid., 199.

3. Klein, *1 Chronicles*, 437.

4. 1 Chr. 28:2, the temple is called "house of rest."

> Lord God, be clothed with salvation and let Your godly
> ones rejoice in what is good.
>
> "O Lord God, do not turn away the face of Your
> anointed; remember Your lovingkindness to Your ser-
> vant David."

2 Chronicles 6:40–42

Solomon's dedication of the temple is mostly repeated word for word, except for the last few verses (1 Kgs. 8:50b–53) which is replaced by this text here 2 Chr. 6:40–42 in which Solomon quotes Ps. 132:8–10.

It has been suggested that "rest" is used differently in the two texts; Sara Japhet argues that "rest" for the Chronicler is thought of primarily as the Ark of the Covenant coming to rest, whereas the psalmist thinks of God resting.[5] To be sure, the Ark finding a resting place is of interest to the Chronicler (1 Chr. 6:31), yet the Chronicler's theology of rest goes beyond this and there does not seem to be a need to separate the two.

Actually though 2 Chr. 6:41–42 is considered in its handling of the psalm. Whereas in the book of Kings, Solomon speaks of God being faithful to his word spoken to his servant Moses (1 Kgs. 8:53), the Chronicler replaces this with the psalmist's request for God to remember his promise to his servant David. The temple as God's resting place and the promise of messianic rest are overlaid; being united by the promise of God's word. Consequently the rest of Solomon's temple points forward to the rest resulting from God's faithfulness to the Davidic covenant.

Another motif prominent in Chronicles, is that of "seeking the Lord." This phrase comes up only a handful of times elsewhere in the Old Testament, whereas in Chronicles the idea of setting one's soul to seek the Lord is a key theme.[6] Keeping God's word is very much entailed within this idea of seeking the Lord with all your heart; for instance when David explains to the Levites why Uzzah died in touching the Ark he says "because you did not carry

---

5. Japhet, *1 and 2 Chronicles: A Commentary*, 603.

6. Hicks, *1 and 2 Chronicles*, 26.

it at the first, the Lord our God made an outburst on us, for we did not seek Him according to the ordinance" (1 Chr. 15:13).

In 2 Chr. 15, the prophet Azariah speaks God's word urging King Asa to seek him and to turn back to the Torah (2 Chr. 15:3). Asa and the people of Israel respond through a covenantal oath accompanied by sacrifice and praise; "all Judah rejoiced concerning the oath, for they had sworn with their whole heart and had sought Him earnestly, and He let them find Him. So the Lord gave them rest on every side" (2 Chr. 15:15). Once more, this time in Chronicles, rest is understood as resulting from obedience to God's word.

A Suitable Conclusion

More than the above observations which highlight the connection between God's word and his rest in Chronicles, this truth is perhaps most clearly observed in the concluding verses of Chronicles. Chronicles of course ends with the people going into exile and the Chronicler emphasizes that this was in order that the land might enjoy its Sabbath rest in accordance with God's word:

> Those who had escaped from the sword he (Nebuchadnezzar) carried away to Babylon; and they were servants to him and to his sons until the rule of the kingdom of Persia, to fulfill the word of the Lord by the mouth of Jeremiah, until the land had enjoyed its sabbaths. All the days of its desolation it kept Sabbath until seventy years were complete.
>
> Now in the first year of Cyrus king of Persia—in order to fulfill the word of the Lord by the mouth of Jeremiah—the Lord stirred up the spirit of Cyrus king of Persia, so that he sent a proclamation throughout his kingdom, and also *put it* in writing, saying, "Thus says Cyrus king of Persia, 'The Lord, the God of heaven, has given me all the kingdoms of the earth, and He has appointed me to build Him a house in Jerusalem, which is in Judah. Whoever there is among you of all His people, may the Lord his God be with him, and let him go up!'"
>
> 2 Chronicles 36:20–23

In this, the ending of Chronicles, God's word takes center stage; the Babylonians ransack the temple, killing Israelites as they go because God's word was repeatedly rejected (2 Chr. 36:15–19). The Israelites remain in exile until a given time, in order to fulfill God's word.[7] Then they later return to Jerusalem and build the temple, so that God's word might be fulfilled. God's word achieves its purpose and there is an inevitability about it, what God has said will come to pass and in as much as the fulfillment of God's word is sure, so is his rest because it is the promised fulfillment of his word.

Did the Chronicler suppose God's eternal rest to be established in the return from exile and rebuilding of the temple? The answer is a resounding "no." As has already been seen, the Chronicler points to a rest to come through the messiah's rule. More than this though it is very clear that the post-exilic community rebuilding the temple did not consider themselves to be living in a time of rest but rather of distress (Neh. 9:37). Ezra's prayer in Neh. 9 is indeed interesting because even though the temple had just been rebuilt, it is a prayer of confession and a petition for mercy. In it Ezra points to the historical reality of disobedience leading to distress and cries of repentance leading to compassion and God's rest (Neh. 9:26–27), placing themselves within this paradigm as those crying out to God in distress having been disobedient.

It is clear then, given the internal evidence from Chronicles itself and the external evidence from texts written around the same time, that the Chronicler did not consider the story to be complete.[8] God's word is still to be completely fulfilled and that is how

---

7. It has been suggested that Chronicles actually finished at 2 Chr. 36:21, which would make the Sabbath rest as a fulfillment of God's word the last verse (Williamson, *Israel in the Book of Chronicles*, 7). The suggestion being that 2 Chr. 36:22–23 were added to bring continuity and nicely join Ezra-Nehemiah to the end of Chronicles, for the last verses of Chronicles are repeated at the beginning of Ezra (Ez. 1:1–3). This is perhaps possible given that the ending of Chronicles seems rather abrupt, yet the supposed addition is entirely consistent with what goes before; making explicit the hope of 2 Chr. 36:21, that there would be a retur (Thompson, *1 and 2 Chronicles*, 392).

8. Selman, *2 Chronicles*, 271.

the Chronicler ends his work.[9] The direction of the Old Testament continues to look forward to the coming eternal rest; a rest inaugurated by the coming king whose rule will be eternal and where warring nations will cease and turn to worship the living God.

9. These verses of Chronicles conclude not only the book as a whole but also the canon in the ordering found in the BHS. The words of Jesus in Matt. 23:35 evidence the earlier existence of this canonical ordering (Bruce, *Canon of Scripture*, 31). Within this structure it is by no means clear why the canon should finish with the book of Chronicles, as chronologically it makes sense for Ezra-Nehemiah to follow Chronicles. One possible reason could be to form an inclusio between Gen. 1–2:3 and 2 Chr. 36:20–23, around God's word and the Sabbath.

Conclusion

This short study has attempted to show that the Old Testament holds to a theology of rest, which is comparable to and yet distinct from that held by their surrounding nations. Of course one of these distinctive features of rest in the Old Testament is that it conceives of rest along its primarily linear view of time, in contrast to the cyclical view held by the nations. Rest has no small part to play in this; it is the defining quality of God's world prior to the fall and it is the defining quality of the eventual new creation. Within these two bookends framing the metanarrative are the stories which prefigure the ending to come. The more dominant stories or strands within the metanarrative are defined by the hoped for restoration of God's eternal rest; notably Israel's conquest of the land, the construction of the temple and the expectation of the coming son of David. These stories run parallel to one another yet their ultimate culmination is never understood to have taken place, pointing as they do to the eternal rest which God will one day establish.

The study has also sought to demonstrate that the Old Testament's theology of rest had missiological implications for the Israelites, in that it provided them with a message for the nations. Even from the early existence of Israel's protohistory and Sabbath observance through to the Song of Moses, the conquest of the land and beyond, Israel's theology of rest was held out as a message for the nations. On numerous occasions throughout the study, the missional implications of Israel's rest have been noted. An increasing amount of scholarship is being produced concerning the subject of mission in the Old Testament and it is hoped that this research will make a positive contribution to it.

With this said it is important to consider what the implications of "rest" are for the church's life and witness.

Though rest is not the central theme shaping unbelievers' worldviews today, it is still a pertinent topic. The consequence of the fall and of sin is that men must toil and know the absence of God's rest. The Sabbath still has a key role and function in the Church's witness for this reason. It is important for the Church to recognize and teach that the Sabbath is not merely a day set for a person to get refreshed; doing something they would not otherwise do in order to be reenergized for the following week. Occasionally it is possible to hear a person talk of when they take "their" day of rest or what they do on "their" day of rest, but the Sabbath is ultimately "the Lord's day" and it is "his" rest which individuals are invited into. The Sabbath is a day of thinking ahead to, and to some extent experiencing, this eternal rest to come while at the same time inviting others to join in.

It is the case that most Christians celebrate the Sabbath on a Sunday, remembering of course Jesus' resurrection from the dead and the life that is to be found in him. This is entirely appropriate as the Old Testament itself expects God's rest to be actualized through the person and work of the messiah; looking ahead to his glorious resting place. This provides Christians with a mandate to explain that God's rest is achieved through the free gift of grace found in the death and resurrection of Jesus.

Another implication that should not be missed is the fact that God's rest is freely given, it is not earned. Just as the nations then thought of rest as something to be achieved or earned through their actions, similarly today people often have the mindset that the toil of this life can be overcome through their own effort. What a fantastic aspect of the gospel message it is then that God's rest is offered freely to all people. It is quite possible to shape the presentation of the gospel message and wider metanarrative paying special attention to this rest, and it may well be a suitable way of presenting the gospel to those offering their busy lives to the idols of money and materialism in an attempt to earn rest.

With the Old Testament's message of rest considered, there is a need, lastly, to review the topics that have arisen in the space of argument which are deserving of further study.

Some readers may wonder why the study did not continue to look at rest through the intertestamental period and into the New Testament. Certainly there are echoes of the Old Testament's message of rest which reverberate into the New, yet the situation is profoundly different; the significance of rest within Greek and Roman thought is not analogous to that of ancient Mesopotamia. The task of researching the question of how the New Testament picks up this theology of rest is sufficiently different from this study's, which was to demonstrate that Israel did indeed have a theology of rest.

Such further study would of course need to look at the way in which the books of Hebrews and Revelation make use of the Old Testament on this point and certainly Jesus' offer of rest would need to be considered. Of course Jesus himself invited people saying:

> Come to me, all you that are weary and are carrying heavy burdens, and I will give you rest. Take my yoke upon you, and learn from me; for I am gentle and humble in heart, and you will find rest for your souls. For my yoke is easy, and my burden is light.
>
> Matthew 11:28–30

Significantly, in these verses Jesus claims to offer rest, which in the Old Testament is something given only by God.

Building upon the theology of rest having missional implications, additional areas for further research would include analysis of the way Israel uses the holy mountain motif, where God takes the place of Baal enthroned on his resting place over the chaos of the waters. There would seem to be space to explore how the Hebrews utilized such language and with what intention.

God's rest will certainly come, even as his words inviting all peoples to receive it have certainly been spoken. That which the Lord has spoken will surely come to pass.

Bibliography

Alter, Robert. *The Art of Biblical Narrative*. New York: Basic, 1983.

Assmann, Jan. *The Mind of Egypt: History and Meaning in the Time of the Pharaohs*. Cambridge: Harvard University Press, 2003.

Averbeck, Richard. "Tabernacle." In *Dictionary of the Old Testament: Pentateuch*, edited by Desmond Alexander and David Baker, 807–27. Downers Grove, IL: InterVarsity, 2003.

Bakon, Shimon. "Centralization of Worship." *Jewish Bible Quarterly* 26.1 (1998) 26–33.

Baldwin, Joyce. *Daniel*. Tyndale Old Testament Commentaries. Downers Grove, IL: InterVarsity, 2009.

Beal, Lissa M. Wray. *1 and 2 Kings*. Downers Grove, IL: InterVarsity, 2014.

Blackburn, W. Ross. *The God Who Makes Himself Known: The Missionary Heart of the Book of Exodus*. Nottingham: InterVarsity, 2012.

Blenkinsopp, Joseph. "The Structure of P," *Catholic Biblical Quaterly* 38 (1976) 275–92.

Block, Daniel. *Deuteronomy*. Grand Rapids: Zondervan, 2012.

———. "Eden: A Temple? A Reassessment of the Biblical Evidence." In *From Creation to New Creation: Biblical Theology and Exegesis*, edited by Daniel Gurtner and Benjamin Gladd, 3–29. Peabody, MA: Hendrickson, 2013.

Braun, Roddy. *1 Chronicles*. Milton Keynes, UK: Paternoster, 1987.

Bruce, Frederick. *The Canon of Scripture*. Downers Grove, IL: InterVarsity, 1988.

Brueggemann, Walter. *Genesis*. Louisville, KY: Westminster John Knox, 2010.

Bush, Frederick. *Ruth-Esther*. Nashville: Thomas Nelson, 1996.

Butler, Trent. *Judges*. Nashville: Thomas Nelson, 2010.

Cassuto, Umberto. *From Adam to Noah: A Commentary on the Book of Genesis, Part 1*. Jerusalem: Magnes, 1978.

Charles, Robert. *The Apocrypha and Pseudopigrapha of the Old Testament: Volume 2*. Oxford: Clarendon, 1963.

Clifford, Richard J. *The Cosmic Mountain in Canaan and the Old Testament*. Cambridge: Harvard University Press, 1972.

Cogan, Mordecai. *1 Kings*. New Haven, CT: Yale University Press, 2008.

Cole, Ross. "The Sabbath and Genesis 2:1–3." *Andrews University Seminary Studies* 41.1 (2003) 5–12.

Craigie, Peter C. *The Book of Deuteronomy*. Grand Rapids: Eerdmans, 1995.

Cross, Frank Moore. *Canaanite Myth and Hebrew Epic: Essays in the History of the Religion of Israel*. Cambridge: Harvard University Press, 1997.

Crusemann, Frank. *The Torah: Theology and Social History of Old Testament Law*. Translated by Allan Mahnke. London: T&T Clark, 1996.

Currid, John D. *Ancient Egypt in the Old Testament*. Grand Rapids: Baker, 1997.

Davies, Philip R. "Sons of Cain." In *A Word in Season: Essays in Honour of William McKane*, edited by James D. Martin and Philip R. Davies. JSOT Supplement 42. Sheffield: Sheffield Academic, 1986.

Day, John. *God's Conflict with the Dragon and the Sea: Echoes of a Canaanite Myth in the Old Testament*. Cambridge: Cambridge University Press, 1985.

De Vaux, Roland. *Ancient Israel: Its Life and Institutions*. London: Darton, Longman & Todd, 1961.

Doukhan, Jacques B. *Genesis Creation Story: Its Literary Structure*. Berrien Springs, MI: Andrews University Press, 1982.

Duguid, Iain. "But Did They Live Happily Ever After? Eschatology in the Book of Esther." *Westminster Theological Journal* 68 (2006) 85–98.

Evans, Mary J. *1 and 2 Samuel*. Peabody, MA: Hendrickson, 2003.

Exum, Cheryl. "The Centre Cannot Hold: Thematic Instabilities in the Book of Judges." *Catholic Biblical Quarterly* 52 (1990) 410–31.

Fishbane, Michael. *Biblical Text and Texture: A Literary Reading of Selected Texts*. Oxford: Oneworld, 1998.

Fleming, Daniel. "Mari's Large Public Tent and the Priestly Tent Sanctuary." *Vetus Testamentum* 50.4 (2000) 484–98.

Foley, John Miles, ed. *A Companion to Ancient Epic*. Blackwell Companions to the Ancient World. London: John Wiley & Sons, 2008.

Foster, Benjamin R. *From Distant Days: Myths, Tales and Poetry of Ancient Mesopotamia*. Bethseda, MD: CDL, 1995.

Fdrethaim, Terence E. *Creation, Fall and Flood*. Minneapolis, MN: Augsburg, 1969.

—————. *Exodus: A Bible Commentary for Teaching and Preaching*. Louisville, KY: Westminster John Knox, 1991.

Gage, Warren Austin. *The Gospel of Genesis: Studies in Protology and Eschatology*. Winona Lake, IN: Carpenter, 1984.

Garrett, Duane. *Rethinking Genesis: The Sources and Authorship of the First Book of the Pentateuch*. Fearn: Mentor, 2000.

Gunkel, Hermann. *Schopfung Und Chaos in Urzeit Und Endzeit*. Gottingen: Vandenhoeck and Ruprecht, 1895.

Hallo, William. "New Moons and Sabbaths: A Case-Study in the Contrastive Approach." *Bible and Spade* 9.4 (1980) 101–13.

Hamilton, Victor P. *The Book of Genesis: Chapters 1–17*. Grand Rapids: Eerdmans, 1991.

Hasenfratz, Hans-Peter. "Patterns of Creation in Ancient Egypt." In *Creation in Jewish and Christian Tradition*, edited by Henning Graf Reventlow and Yair Rabbi Hoffman, 174–78. JSOT Supplement 319. Sheffield: Sheffield Academic, 2002.

Heschel, Abraham. *The Sabbath*. New York: Farrar Straus Giroux, 2005.

Hess, Richard S. *Joshua*. Downers Grove, IL: InterVarsity, 2008.

Hicks, John Mark. *1 and 2 Chronicles*. Joplin, Missouri: College, 2001.

Hoffmeier, James K. *Israel in Egypt: The Evidence for the Authenticity of the Exodus Tradition*. Oxford: Oxford University Press, 1999.

Jacob, Benno. *The Second Book of the Bible: Exodus*. Hoboken, NJ: Ktav, 1992.

Japhet, Sara. *1 and 2 Chronicles: A Commentary*. Louisville, KY: Westminster John Knox, 1993.

Jobes, Karen. *Esther*. Grand Rapids: Zondervan, 2011.

Kaiser Jr., Walter. "The Promise Theme and the Theology of Rest." *Bibliothecha Sacra* 130.518 (1973) 135–48.

Kearney, Peter J. "Creation and Liturgy: The P Redaction of Ex. 25–40." *Zeitschrift Fur Alttestamentliche Zeitscrift* 89 (1977) 375–87.

Keel, Othmar. *The Symbolism of the Biblical World: Ancient Near Eastern Iconography and the Book of Psalms*. Translated by Timothy J. Hallett. London: SPCK, 1978.

Keil, Carl Friedrich. *Manual of Biblical Archaeology*. Vol. 1. Edinburgh: T. & T. Clark, 1888.

Kitchen, Kenneth A. *On the Reliability of the Old Testament*. Grand Rapids: Eerdmans, 2003.

Kiuchi, Nobuyoshi. *Leviticus*. Nottingham: InterVarsity, 2007.

Klein, Ralph. *1 Chronicles*. Minneapolis, MN: Augsburg Fortress, 2006.

Koorevaar, Hendrik. *De Opbouw van Het Boek Jozua*. Heverlee: Centrum voor Bijbelse Vorming Belgie, 1990.

Levenson, Jon. "The Temple and the World." *The Journal of Religion* 64.3 (1984) 275–98.

Loewenstamm, S E. "The Seven Day-Unit in Ugaritic Epic Literature." *Israel Exploration Journal* 15.3 (1965) 121–33.

Matthews, Kenneth A. *Genesis 1–11:26*. Nashville: Broadman & Holman, 1996.

McConville, Gordon. *Deuteronomy*. Leicester: InterVarsity, 2002.

McConville, Gordon, and Stephen Williams. *Joshua*. Grand Rapids: Eerdmans, 2010.

Merrill, Eugene. *Deuteronomy*. Nashville: Broadman and Holman, 1994.

———. "Deuteronomy and de Wette: A Fresh Look at a Fallacious Premise." *Journal of the Evangelical Study of the Old Testament* 1.1 (2012) 25–42.

Monson, John. "The Temple of Solomon: Heart of Jerusalem." In *Zion City of Our God*, edited by Richard Hess and Gordon Wenham. Grand Rapids: Eerdmans, 1999.

Motyer, J. Alec. *The Prophecy of Isaiah*. Downers Grove, IL: InterVarsity, 1993.

Ockinga, Boya G., "The Memphite Theology—Its Purpose and Date." In *Egyptian Culture and Society: Studies in Honour of Naguib Kanawati*, Vol.

2, edited by Alexandra Woods, et al., 99–113. Supplement Aux Annales Du Service Des Antiquites de L'egypte 38. Cairo, Egypt: The American University in Cairo Press, 2010.

Oswalt, John N. *The Bible among the Myths*. Grand Rapids: Zondervan, 2009.

———. *The Book of Isaiah: Chapters 40-66*. New International Commentary on the Old Testament. Grand Rapids: Eerdmans, 1998.

Pitkanen, Pekka. *Joshua*. Downers Grove, IL: InterVarsity, 2010.

Ploger, Otto. *Theocracy and Eschatology*. Oxford: Blackwell, 1968.

Reid, Debra. *Esther: An Introduction and Survey*. Downers Grove, IL: InterVarsity, 2008.

Robinson, Gnana. *The Origin and Development of the Old Testament Sabbath: A Comprehensive Exegetical Approach*. Frankfurt: Verlag Peter Lang, 1975.

Rooker, Mark F. *Leviticus*. Nashville: Broadman & Holman, 2000.

Rothenberg, Beno. *Timna: Valley of the Biblical Copper Mines*. New Aspects of Antiquity. London: Thames & Hudson, 1972.

Rubenstein, Jeffrey. "Sukkot, Eschatology and Zechariah 14." *Revue Biblique* 103.2 (1996) 161–95.

Sarna, Nahum M. *Exodus*. Philadelphia, PA: Jewish Publication Society, 1994.

Sasson, Jack. *Judges 1- 12*. New Haven, CT: Yale University Press, 2014.

———. "Word-Play in Genesis 6:8- 9." *Catholic Biblical Quarterly* 37.2 (1975) 165–66.

Schaefer, Konrad. "The Ending of the Book of Zechariah: A Commentary." *Revue Biblique* 100.2 (1993) 165–238.

Selman, Martin. *2 Chronicles*. Downers Grove, IL: InterVarsity, 2008.

Speiser, Ephraim. *Genesis*. New York: Doubleday, 1964.

Spronk, Klaas. *Beatific Afterlife in Ancient Israel and in the Ancient Near East*. Kevelaer: Butzon & Bercker, 1986.

Thompson, John. *1 and 2 Chronicles*. Nashville: Broadman and Holman, 1994.

Timmer, Daniel. *Creation, Tabernacle and Sabbath: The Sabbath Frame of Exodus 31:12-17; 35:1-3 In Exegetical and Theological Perspective*. Göttingen: Vandenhoeck & Ruprecht, 2008.

Toshio Tsumura, David. *The Book of 1 Samuel*. New International Commentary on the Old Testament. Grand Rapids: Eerdmans, 2006.

Tsumura, David Toshio. *Earth and the Waters in Genesis 1 and 2: A Linguistic Investigation*. JSOT Supplement 83. Sheffield: Continuum International, 1989.

VanGemeren, Willem. "'Abba' in the Old Testament?" *Journal of the Evangelical Theological Society* 31.4 (1988) 385–98.

von Rad, Gerhard. *Deuteronomy*. Trowbridge: SCM Press, 1966.

———. *Genesis*. Trowbridge: SCM Press, 1963.

———. *Old Testament Theology*. Vol. 1. 2 vols. Edinburgh: Oliver & Boyd, 1962.

———. *The Problem of the Hexateuch and Other Essays*. Trowbridge: SCM Press, 2012.

Walton, John H. *Ancient Near Eastern Thought and the Old Testament: Introducing the Conceptual World of the Hebrew Bible.* Nottingham: Apollos, 2007.

Watson, Rebecca S. *Chaos Uncreated: A Reassessment of the Theme of "Chaos" in the Hebrew Bible.* Beihefte Zur Zeitschrift Fur Die Alttestamentliche Wissenschaft 314. Berlin: de Gruyter, 2005.

Webb, Barry. *The Book of Judges.* Grand Rapids: Eerdmans, 2012.

Weinfeld, Moshe. *The Promise of the Land: The Inheritance of the Land by the Israelites.* Berkeley: University of California Press, 1993.

Wenham, Gordon J. *The Book of Leviticus.* Grand Rapids: Eerdmans, 1979.

———. "The Coherence of the Flood Narrative." In *I Studied Inscriptions from Before the Flood: Ancient Near Eastern Literary and Linguistic Approaches to Genesis*, edited by Richard S. Hess and David Toshio Tsumura, 436–37. Sources for Biblical and Theological Study. Vol. 4. Winona Lake, IN: Eisenbrauns, 1994.

———. *Genesis 1-15.* Edinburgh: Thomas Nelson, 1987.

———. "The Perplexing Pentateuch." *Vox Evangelica* 17 (1987) 7–22.

———. "Sanctuary Symbolism in the Garden of Eden Story." In *I Studied Inscriptions from Before the Flood: Ancient Near Eastern Literary and Linguistic Approaches to Genesis*, edited by Richard S. Hess and David Toshio Tsumura, 399–404. Sources for Biblical and Theological Study. Vol. 4. Winona Lake, IN: Eisenbrauns, 1994.

Westermann, Claus. *Genesis 1-11.* Minneapolis, MN: Augsburg, 1984.

Williamson, Hugh. *Israel in the Book of Chronicles.* Cambridge: Cambridge University Press, 2007.

Woudstra, Marten H. *The Book of Joshua.* Grand Rapids: Eerdmans, 1981.

Wright, Christopher. *Deuteronomy.* Peabody, MA: Hendrickson, 1996.

———. *Old Testament Ethics for the People of God.* Downers Grove, IL: InterVarsity, 2010.

Young, Edward J. *Studies in Genesis One.* Philadelphia, PA: Presbyterian & Reformed, 1964.